Hotel Guestroom Design

Paula Jo Boykin
Spectrum Services

SPECTRUM
S E R V I C E S

KENDALL/HUNT PUBLISHING COMPANY
2460 Kerper Boulevard P.O. Box 539 Dubuque, Iowa 52004-0539

DISCLAIMER

The information and statements herein are believed to be reliable, but are not to be construed as warranty or representation for which the author or publishers assume legal responsibility. Users should undertake sufficient verification and testing to determine the suitability for their own particular purpose of information or products referred to herein.

For the person in my life who bestowed the gift of grasping life with vigor and enthusiasm, who understood the need for patience, love and guidance in raising a family and who taught me to tackle a career with fortitude and reach for the stars. A profusion of thanks to my late mother, Mary Jo Longo.

Contents

Acknowledgments, vii
Introduction, ix

Chapter 1
Where Do I Begin?, 1
A. Client's Objectives
B. Feasibility Studies
C. Chain or Independent Hotel
D. Specifications As Per Owner/Franchisee

Chapter 2
Shape of Room, 7
A. Components and Amenities of Standard Guestroom
B. Layout
C. Elevations
D. Electrical
E. Reflected Ceiling Plan

Chapter 3
Guestroom Specifications, 13
A. Soft Goods
B. Case Goods
C. Seating
D. Lighting
E. Accessories

Chapter 4
Guestroom Bath Specifications, 27
A. Flooring and Wall Surfaces
B. Lighting
C. Vanity/Tub/Fixtures

Chapter 5
Guestroom Corridors, 33
A. Lighting
B. Signage
C. Elevator Lobbies

Chapter 6
Process, 41
A. Specification Book
B. Finish Schedule
C. Color Board
D. Presentation

Appendix, 49
Addendums
1. Corporate specification example
2. Feasibility summary example
3. Scaled and unscaled drawing
4. Kingroom furniture layout
5. FF&E standard size chart/Estimation of wallcovering and carpet
6. Guestroom elevation
7. Guestroom reflected ceiling and electrical plan
8. Symbols chart
9. Bedspread, coverlette, and dust ruffle styles
10. Bedspread specification sheet
11. Measuring for window treatments
12. Carpet specification
13. Casegood specification
14. Specification sheet example
15. Finish schedules
16. Colorboard example
17. Additional guestroom type layouts
18. Corridor carpet layouts
19. Guestroom signage
20. Renderings

Glossary, 129

Acknowledgments

As a practicing Interior Designer for the last 15 years, I based the need for this type of learning tool for today's Interior Design students on the portfolios I have reviewed in the past. Researching libraries and colleges coast to coast, it was clear to me that there was a true void in the information available to the college student and novice designer.

Hospitality design has taken on a much broader scope than was ever considered before. It requires a more aesthetic attitude towards flow and function and specific attention to detail and design.

This workbook is the *1st* of a series to do more than just scratch the surface of the specialized field of hotel and guestroom design.

As the Hospitality industry grows, hotel guests are becoming more sophisticated, state codes more stringent and the Interior Designer must meet these ever changing challenges.

I would like to extend my thanks to the many friends, family and associates who supported me with their kind words and encouragement in the development of this series.

My very special thanks to three dynamic former and present executive assistants that played a major role in my revisions, Ms. Sondra Walker, Ms. Alice Proctor and Ms. Joanne Putka.

I extend my sincere gratitude to Boykin Management Corporation, hotel developers and operators, who I have maintained as a client for the past 10 years, and to the Marriott and Hilton Corporations, Choice International, all my professional supporters and past and present clients. In addition, a special thanks to Mr. Richard H. Penner, Professor at Cornell University for his time in reviewing my manuscript.

And last a final thanks to Kendall/Hunt Publishers for the patience and support in making my dream become a reality.

Introduction

There are numerous components to designing a hotel facility. It is literally a town within walls. It provides a place for dining, sleeping, entertainment, limited shopping, swimming and exercise, all without leaving the facility. Each of these components have specific objectives, budgets and amenities that are to be provided in the original design. This workbook will concentrate on the many facets of the hotel guestroom design. We will cover layouts and specifications for dressing, bath, living and sleeping areas, concentrate on lighting, floor and wall-coverings, softgoods, casegoods, accessories and window treatments in detail. We will also briefly review corridor design as these are the main arteries to the guestrooms.

All pages including the addendum drawings and charts are perforated for the convenience of using in your notebooks or on your drafting boards.

A designer's dream is to be handed a design project that is starting from scratch. No guidelines, no budget and four blank walls. Unfortunately, it is rare to find this and in most cases, a designer will never experience a project with no parameters. It also lacks challenge, control, initiative and discipline. Anyone could design a lovely guestroom with an open-end budget and no parameters!

There are several types of guestroom projects a designer will be asked to partake in—

1. New Construction

2. Renovation

3. Partial Renovation.

Each type offers pros and cons to it and a variety of changes. We will discuss each of these.

New Construction

A new construction project is one that is in the process of being built. It offers much challenge and a tremendous amount of responsibility by the design team.

Renovation

A total renovation project also offers its challenges, as it limits you in various ways, as you are forced to deal with existing windows, electrical and hardwire fixture locations.

Partial Renovations

A partial renovation offers more challenges than the other two, as it allows you to get very creative in incorporating the old with the new, and determining what stays and what goes.

I have listed on the following page items that you will identify with in each of the above type projects.

New Construction	Renovation	Partial Renovation
Opportunity for any floor plan and electrical plan	Less flexibility with floor plan	Less flexibility with floor plan
Opportunity to be flexible with electrical outlets and to insure adequate coverage	Have to work around existing electrical, structural wall, etc.	Have to work around existing electrical, structural wall, as well as FF&E items not being replaced.
Sample room allows you to rectify any changes you need or want to make	Working in an existing property and having to work around guests and staff. Slim time frame.	Time frame and room availablity restraints.

Regardless of which type reflects your guestroom design project, similarities such as layout, color palette, lighting, finishes and presentation will always be part of your design project.

The following pages will help to prepare you for your clients expectations, and it will assist you in turning over a quality design project from beginning to completion.

Remember your goal is to meet your client's objectives!

Chapter One

Where Do I Begin?

Client's Objective's

Where do you begin? You've been given the assignment to develop a conceptual standard guestroom design for a franchise owner of a full service hotel. Before any layouts, drawings or **specifications** can begin, it is imperative that you have the objectives of the hotel owner in writing. If it is a franchise hotel managed by a professional management group, it is essential that their objectives be coupled with the owner's to insure your client's demands are met, and to enable you to perform your job to the very best of your ability. Communication is always of the utmost importance, and it is a skill you will need to develop and utilize throughout your design career.

Feasibility Study

Before beginning your design project, it is imperative that the following questions be addressed to your client or be included in the owner's written objectives. Whenever possible, request a copy of a **feasibility study** (one should be done in the development stages) to review. This study usually offers pertinent information relating to the area competition, and the physical look and style of the intended hotel site/structure—external and internal.

A specification book is usually provided with regard to design limitations and restrictions. You can always exceed in specifications and usually obtain corporate approval. But, if an item does not meet corporate/owner specifications, it will rarely be approved for the design. You must always familiarize yourself with state and city codes in regard to fire hazards, handicapped people, environmental standards, etc. These requirements are equally as important as those of your client; to disregard them, or be ignorant of them can prove to be a very costly mistake.

Chain or Independent Hotel

1. Determine type of hotel. (1) Full Service (2) Budget (3) Resort (4) other

2. Is it a franchise label or private?

3. What is the size of the hotel and its components?

4. Total budget of hotel? Separate the **Furniture, Fixtures and Equipment** (F.F.&E.) cost per component.

    Example: Guestroom Furniture, Fixture

and Equipment Budget	$300,000
Corridor Budget	$100,000
Public Space Budget	$275,000

5. List the number of standard guestrooms.

   List the number of suites.

   Is there a concierge or executive level? List number of each type of guestrooms involved.

   List the number of king rooms, double/double rooms, parlors, and queens.

6. Request a full set of drawings from the architect that includes layouts of guestroom wings, **connecting door** and bath locations. Request window wall **elevations**. Pay close attention to bearing walls, any electrical wiring that may be located prior to your input, sprinkler locations and handicapped accessibilities and designated room locations.

7. If property is a franchise hotel, request a copy of all specifications pertaining to your project (see Add. 1 for examples of a corporate drapery specification from several different hotels). As a **franchise** property, specifications should be available to you that will dictate much of your design specifications, i.e., carpet, vinyl and fabric weight, casegoods, and numerous other items in your design.

8. Get preferences from the owner/operator. Is there a theme that will prevail through the hotel: contemporary, traditional, rustic eclectic? Is there a preference in color?

9. Request time frames for the completion of the following:
   a. Preliminary design, budget and layouts.

   b. Renderings and elevations.

   c. Completion of color boards and specification books.

   d. Presentation to owners/operators

   e. Presentation to franchise group.

   f. Bidding process (if you are involved in purchasing).

   g. Installation of FF&E.

10. The results of the feasibility study will answer many questions (see Add. 2 for example). In the event one is not available, the following questions need answers:
    a. Type of guest:
       1. Business Traveler—A work area and comfortable chair with adequate lighting essential.
       2. Vacationing families—FF&E durability, flexibility in room layout to offer space for daybed or convertible sofa with a residential feel are prime concerns.

3. High-end Corporate or Resort Hotel—The logistics, climate, theme and budget per room will dictate how elaborate the design will be.

b. What is the intended stay of the traveler? If the business person is to be of primary concern, common sense dictates that he will be a short-term guest. Vacationers and resort hotels will cater to the long-term guest, and the Corporate Hotel will cater to V.I.P.'s and people mixing business with pleasure. This will determine clothing and luggage storage needs.

c. What is the percentage of female travelers?—Would this warrant a secured floor? Better lighting in bath area and built-in amenities such as hair dryers are considerations.

d. If an executive level is intended before beginning the project, it would be wise to get a list of intended amenities in order to include proper electrical wiring, lighting and design needs. Are electronic shoe shiners, remote control televisions, night lights, refrigerators, or mini bars to be a part of your design?

e. If executive suites or parlors are to be part of your guestroom mix, what will be the maximum occupancy in this room? Will there be F&B service and board room set up? Will furniture continually be moved around for banquet setups?

f. The budget has a way of dictating the elegance or economy approach to guestroom design. What are the restraints on the bath areas? Plastic laminate, marble, or corian counters? Prefab acrylic tub enclosures or cast iron? Tile or vinyl flooring? Specialty **amenities**, such as jaccuzies, stall showers, etc.?

g. Percentage of intended room service in guestroom will dictate research on appropriate seating and lighting.

Chapter 1 Quiz

1. List two items that dictate the quality of the guestroom design.

2. Name three other items to include on your objective list—Addendum 1 will help in the preliminary stage of your design.

3. Read the attached feasibility study (Add. 2) give <u>5</u> items that will aid you in your design efforts and explain why.

4. What does FF&E mean?

5. What similarities do you see in the corporate supplied specifications given in Addendum 1?

Chapter Two

Shape of Room

Standard Guestroom

The shape of the guestroom is based on architectural drawings which are always drawn to scale. If you have not worked in scale, that is to say, used a scale rule, it is important that you closely review Addendum 3, Example 2, where three different scales are shown 1/2", 1/4" and 1/8". The most commonly used scale is 1/4" = 1'. Using a **scale** rule allows you to condense your drawing to a much smaller size. As an exercise, use a single guestroom drawing from each guestroom category and enlarge it to at least a 1/4" scale so you can work on each individual layout (see Addendum 3). Check with your instructor if you are not sure of your scale drawing or measurements. It's good practice to use tracing paper as an overlay and develop a variety of layouts before making your decision; definitely prior to beginning specifying and drafting. Be efficient with your time and be creative with your energies.

Layout

The objectives received from the client will determine the type of furnishing you will select. Addendum 4 is based on an actual guestroom at Marriott's Tenaya Lodge at Yosemite in Fish Camp, California. This is a resort hotel, with an average guest stay of three days. Using Marriott criteria and suggested layouts, it was determined that in the majority of king rooms, the bed was to have lighting on both sides. Options were: (1) free standing lamp or (2) wall mounted lamps. Other objectives were to provide a work area, dining area, comfortable seating and adequate dresser space.

This particular room measures 13' × 28' which is a common size guestroom for hotels. The size of this particular guestroom is generous, but it is not large enough to accommodate both a desk and separate dining table.

This layout suggests the use of an over-sized desk, 4' wide and 2 1/2 feet long × 29" high, that would also be used for in-suite dining. This hotel has a high percentage of corporate clients and vacationers. It was estimated that the room service would be in the mid-range percentile, and the high percent of corporate clients dictated the need for a suitable work space/table, good lighting and telephone accessability. Be sure that the design of the desk you select won't interfere with the chair that will be used. Some desks have supports on the underside that make it impossible for a chair to be pushed underneath on both sides.

A comfortable chair (with or without ottoman) is an added attraction and imparts a residential feel to the room and a sense of relaxation to a weary traveler. Again, lighting plays an important role as does a table near the chair. A six drawer credenza rather than a four drawer can be used (check your objectives or feasibility study for the average night stay for guests) and offer extra storage space. In the case of Addendum 4, we've opted for an oversized armoire, that not only features six large drawers, but also accommodates the T.V., in-room safe and mini refrigerator.

The question that needs to be addressed is what is the average stay of the hotel guest? Extended stays would certainly warrant a credenza with more space, as the closet is limited. Although mirrors are normally used over the credenza, if you can add mirror doors, bifolding or sliding, to the closet area, it will add depth and light to the entry area. Keep in mind that when choosing an armoire over a credenza, that the only available area for mirrors, outside of the bathroom area, would be on the closet doors.

The bed size is determined by the **room mix** designation from the client, king, queen or full. Be aware that there is more than one size for a king bed. Refer to the chart on Addendum 5 for frequently used sizes. These charts can be referred to often for use in estimation purposes in drawing layouts, elevations, or developing bid packages. All items naturally should be field measured when working on an existing hotel and refurbishing existing furnishings. A registered **template** of bed sizes is extremely helpful and can be purchased from the offices of the American Society of Interior Designers (ASID) in Washington, D.C.

Elevations

Once your furniture layout is approved and your measurements are accurate, you should move on to the elevations of each wall. In Addendum 4, the square with a circle insert symbol is used to designate each individual wall in the room. Addendum 6 is an elevation of wall #4. An elevation is a flat scale drawing of the rear, side or front of a building or interior.

Electrical

What is the purpose of this exercise? First of all, the elevation drawing is to scale, so you can determine if the furnishings fit the space. Is the piece too wide? Too short? Does it have adequate clearance for cords, bedspreads, etc.? This can all be determined by your elevation drawings. Placement of furnishings, pictures and mirrors, wall mounted headboard cleats, lighting, etc. are also determined by this drawing. It is an essential reference for whomever is handling the installation of the guestroom. It functions as a cross-reference, as it identifies the location of lamps, televisions, clocks, and other electrical accessories, and also assists in identifying electrical outlets and the exact location for **hardwire**/electrical fixtures. Refer to Addendum 7 for electrical outlet locations and telephone **jacks**. Using a tissue overlay, practice and develop an alternate electrical plan.

Reflected Ceiling Plan

Addendum 7 represents the **reflected ceiling** plan for the same guestroom used in Addendum 4. A separate reflected ceiling plan is not necessary unless a lay-in-grid ceiling is used or a substantial amount of ceiling light fixtures are hardwired. It is an excellent tool to use to determine where sprinkler heads are to be located (normally the responsibility of the architects). Refer to Addendum 8 for appropriate and common symbols when drafting guestrooms.

When preparing your electrical locations in your guestroom, use the following check list:

A. Determine if a 1-2-3 plug should be specified.

B. Did you allow ample and **convenience outlets** for housekeeping?

C. Were appropriate jacks installed for phone, desk and/or nightstand location?

D. If separate alarm clock is a standard specification, determine location and electrical outlet.

E. Review all lamp locations to verify electrical outlet source. For example, if the budget is a problem, and one outlet has to be centered behind the king headboard, be certain you specify a custom cord length for your lamp.

F. If hardwire mounts apply to your guestroom design, accurately determine exact location for **J-Box** and mounting brackets. Please note: Direct wire offers little or no flexibility when room is renovated, or if furniture layouts are changed. This is more important when designing suites, because the floor plans have more options than standard guestrooms.

Carefully review the final architectural drawings to verify that all of the electrical locations you requested have been included in the final set of architectural drawings.

At this point, your room layout is complete with "generic" furnishings. The elevations verify furniture placement in relationship to the walls, and your reflected ceiling plan and electrical layout cross-references assure you that this furniture should fit and adequate electrical has been addressed. Now we will move on to color, textures, finishes and product specifications needed to produce a finished guestroom.

Chapter 2 Quiz

1. Using an overlay for the "B" Suite in Addendum 4, develop a layout that includes two full size beds, instead of a king.

2. Utilizing the layouts above, draw an electrical plan that will meet the needs of your new layout.

3. Using Addendum 6 as an example, develop wall elevations for all the walls in your layout.

4. Estimate the square footage needed for Addendum 4 Suite with 8 ft. ceilings in the following areas. Refer to Addendum 5 for formulas.

   a. Wallcovering for guestroom (lineal yards)

   b. Wallcovering for bath (in rolls)

   c. Carpeting (square feet)

5. List the following bed sizes:

   a. California King   _____

   b. Regular King   _____

   c. Queen   _____

   d. Double   _____

   e. Twin   _____

   f. Youth-Bed   _____

   g. Roll-Away Bed   _____

Chapter Three

Guestroom Specifications

Soft Goods

While each designer has his or her own system or technique to begin specifications and design of hotel guestrooms, experience has proven that it is more efficient to begin with the bedspread specification. The bedspread is a highly abused item in hospitality design. It is sat on, stepped on, eaten on and patrons will even shine their shoes with it. With so many possibilities of soil, it makes very good sense to spec a fabric that not only is durable but that has a pattern that is busy enough to hide some of the obvious stains, soil and cigarette burns. Obviously this is your opportunity to select your color scheme because all the other fabrics and textures will be coordinated around the bedspread fabric. When a bedspread looks soiled or faded in appearance, it makes the entire room look old and/or unkept. This is your single most important specification, as it represents the largest source of color and design in the room, with the exception of the carpet.

The most common spec for a bedspread fabric is one that is printed on a 100% warped cotton sateen. It is made of strong cotton fibers that hold up to repeated washings and holds the color fastness quite well. You'll find that most middle to high end hotel chains will use the 100% warped cotton sateen specification. Your more budget properties will specify a 50% cotton/50% polyester gray goods to print on. The 50/50 blend can save as much as 30% per yard when purchased in volume and when compared to the 100% warped cotton sateen cost. They both hold up quite well under normal wear, though the 50/50 blend is a limper fabric and has much less nap to it.

To increase longevity of a bedspread, quilting should be added as it helps the spread maintain it's look and shape. An 8 ounce polyester fill with a 4–6'' **channel quilting** (quilted in horizontal or vertical stripes), throw spread with round corners is a normal specification for a standard hotel guestroom spread. Backed with a cotton backing, it offers hotel operations longevity and easy maintenance. Outline quilting (outlines all shapes in the pattern) is an exceptionally handsome treatment but is usually difficult to include into a realistic budget. Refer to Addendum 9 for additional quilting and bed spread styles and a sample bedspread specification.

Because bed bases, frames and thickness of mattresses and boxsprings vary slightly from manufacturer to manufacturer, it is imperative that these be field measured prior to ordering because the bedspread drops can vary.

Whether the fabric be a bold colorful print or a small mini print, it is wise to stay away from patterns that have a lot of solid, negative space, especially if it is of a neutral, light color.

Reserve these fabrics for tropical and high-end resorts where the spreads are changed more frequently, as the solids and neutrals will show wear much sooner than a vivid colored fabric.

Once the bedspread fabric is selected, the next step is to select a fabric for your over-drapery that coordinates and compliments the bedspread in color and pattern. Many of your large cotton prints offer coordinating smaller geometrics, stripes, etc., which are very interesting and if acceptable, can help to shorten your research in locating your overdrapery fabric. Should you not choose to select the coordinating fabric, your objective should be to make your drapery specification look like it should be a coordinate. Keep in mind the draperies (overs and unders) are handled often by housekeeping staff and guests. The soilage from just the natural skin oils can produce marks. Therefore, color and pattern on the overdrapery fabric should be a priority when specifying.

In most cases your client or corporate franchise will determine if a stationary side panel or a full over drape is to be used in the guestroom. The single stationary panel usually 30'' in width, has been quite prevalant in the past and is considered quite economical. The disad-vantage of this drapery treatment is that when used on a sliding glass door for example, it has a tendency to appear lop-sided, as many times the panel used only on the stationary side of the sliding door.

Full over draperies with a center draw or one way draw add much more plushness and residential feel to the guestroom if the budget allows for it. Valances are used to top off a window treatment when you are designing for a mid to high-end hotel facility, but they are not necessary in a standard guestroom unless specified by the owner and/or franchise.

One of the biggest complaints by hotel guests is when light escapes through the drapery overlap or **returns** and doesn't provide 100% privacy from the outside. To prevent this, a **blackout** liner is essential in all guestroom installations. This is the under drape closest to the window that runs the full length and width of the window with adequate overage to seal out daylight. Generally, this fabric is a rubberized type vinyl on one side with a suede or felt like nap on the other side. The latter side faces the window. The black out drapery is characterized by manufacturers as an insulated type of fabric. As it is a heavy fabric, it is not recommended to laminate a full overdrape with it. If the overdrape specification is considerably lighter in weight, it will work as a lining that's attached at the header (top) of the drape and not at the hemline. The blackout fabric is a bulky fabric and when used as a lining can produce bellowed pleats. When the application calls for a full drape, there are other acceptable weights that work successfully when lining an overdrape.

Often, in standard guestrooms, a sheer drapery is used between the blackout (when it is a separate drape) and overdrape or side panel. This can be an opaque or transparent fabric (usually in a neutral off white hue). It is the same size as the separate blackout liner, hung on the second rod, closest to the window. The blackout, (when separate from the overdrape), and sheer drape, should be 1/2'' shorter in length than the overdrape. Review Addendum 11 for suggested measuring techniques.

One-way drawdrapes and traverse overdraperies that pull to one side of the window or glass door, offer benefits to those windows/doors opening to one side. Having your drapery stack back to the opposite side of the opening will prevent soilage on the draperies and the possibility of them being caught in the window or door as they are opened or closed.

When specifying one-way draw drapes, don't forget to consider the **stack back** area re-quired to allow enough glass exposure when drapes are opened. It is wise to extend the draperies beyond the actual window size. A good rule of thumb to determine how much your stack back will amount to is:

Formula:

Double Fullness—Divide width of glass area by 6 and add this amount to each side of the window.

2–1/2 Fullness—Divide width of glass area by 5 and add this amount to each side of the window.

Triple Fullness—Divide width of glass area by 4 and add this amount to each side of the window.

Example:

Window is 48″ wide and we are specifying a drape with a double fullness:
48 ÷ 6 = 8″ of stack back on each side of a 48″ window.

  8″ /   48″   / 8″ × 48″ Length

This formula will help you determine if the stack back takes up too much room on your pane of glass, blocking visibility or if you have enough room to go beyond the window and have the drapery stack back on the wall to offer full window exposure when the draperies are open. To take this a step further, review the example below to determine actual size drapery needed for this window.

(Stack Back on Wall)   8″ /   48″   / 8″   (Stack Back on Wall)

Size of Glass	= 48″
Total Stack Back	= 16″
3″ on Each Side of Return and 3″ on Each Side of Overlap	= 12″
Actual width size of drape	76″

The finished width of 76″ is for a single over drape on a window. Should a sheer be underneath, your overall width changes to a plus 6″, thus totaling 82″ width.

Now we move on to the next specification for our hotel room. Second to the bedspread and drapes, carpet is our next concern. Durability is the main objective here. Hotel/franchise owners have their own thoughts as to what type of carpet be used in their guestrooms. The following checklist will enable you to narrow down manufacturers that can offer you what you are working for in completing a correct specification for your project.

What kind of texture are you looking for:
- Level Loop
- Multi-Level
- Plush

What kind of yarn:
- Wool
- Nylon
- Acrylic
- Olefin

Type of Traffic Patterns:
- Light
- Medium
- Heavy

Hotel Maintenance Program:
- In-house program or independent.
- Percentage of room service to allow for spillage.
- Are there rooms on street level?; off carpeted corridors?; outside entries?; sun exposure in rooms?
- Be aware of fire codes in local area.
- Weight of carpet needed (28–32 ounce common in mid price hotel rooms.
- Installation: Type: Over/Pad (sponge rubber, foam rubber, urethan foam) or direct glue down to floor surface. (Note the latter, direct glue down is usually used in public or Food and Beverage areas, where there is cart traffic, as opposed to a large percentage of foot traffic.) A double glue pad is also another choice for heavy cart traffic.

Guidelines for Measuring Carpet

Once the carpet is specified, the designer will rely on the purchasing or installation expert to come up with a figure. However, if you are responsible for the budget, it is good to know how to come up with "ball park" figures for an estimate. Keep in mind the following items:

- Find out repeat of pattern if applicable.
- Carpet seam placement will dictate necessary overages.
- Nap should run in same direction which will also dictate possible overage.
- Many hoteliers prefer an additional amount of carpet to be ordered for patching, etc, which should be calculated in bid. A 10% overage will usually suffice.

One very important item to remember is to *Never order any quantities based on your "estimates"*. Have the contractor/installer determine the quantities, whether it be by a physical measurement or the measuring of blue prints in the case of new construction.

Carpet salesmen and installers can offer you valuable information regarding the strengths and weaknesses of different types of carpet fibers, installation factors, etc. Take advantage of their knowledge and day to day involvement with the product.

I have found that a plush, low pile, dense 32-ounce nylon carpet is a durable specification for most middle to high end guestrooms. More and more designers are using small tone-on-tone geometric prints, pindots or moresque (various colors of yarns, twisted to create a textured, muted color) carpets in hotel guestrooms. Why you ask, when a solid plush goes with everything? Because the shading of the prints or speckle design makes the hotel guest less likely to notice the wear and fading. In addition, a subtle tufted, patterned carpet helps minimize traffic patterns. Remember, you have a lot of fabric patterns going on in the room. Carpet that has a pattern with a mild contrast incolation, or a textured appearance, can be quite appealing and offer the longevity your hotel owner is looking for. Budgets dictate the quality of your carpet. The larger the carpet budget, the more affordable carpet per yard can be considered for your specification. And, the larger the order the better cost will be to the Hotelier. When you are comparing costs of different manufacturers, make certain you are comparing "apples to apples". Review the total specifications of each carpet selection to determine if a same or similar carpet is being considered. For an example of a carpet specification, see Addendum 12 and note the detailed information offered.

This specification, for example, would be utilized by the purchaser to seek competitive bids. The installer will also find this information to be quite valuable in determining seaming, pad specifications, etc. The maintenance department will also use this specification, because it will give them the best type of cleaning method to use on this particular carpet. Another party that will find these specifications very useful is the individual/organization who is approving the design. In conclusion, it's very important to include pertinent information regarding the product so all individuals will be aware of its capabilities.

Casegoods

Casegoods are usually termed in the hospitality lingo as furnishings with a wood or hard-material type frame. Examples are dresser, nightstands, headboards, wood chairs, wood framed mirrors, (which can also be classified as an accessory), armoires, etc. While "soft good" renovations are done on a fairly frequent basis by hoteliers, the hardgoods or casegoods are specified with longevity in mind. Specifying a casegood that is structurally sound is as important as finding one that will not be dated in design.

For example, hotel guestrooms that are located in warm climates, have a "natural" material available to them, i.e., rattan furniture. The timeless "tropical vacation" look makes it very suitable for the area, and the style can be designed for a low to high-end design. In the midwest area, though, a rattan casegood design would look out of place. In addition, a contemporary style of furnishings that was well received in 1976, would not be acceptable in the early '80s. Traditional styled furniture that is basic, not overly elaborate in detailing and has a rich wood tone, is usually a "safe" specification. Regardless of the exterior design of the casegoods, it is imperative that a good specification is written to ensure the quality and dependability that is needed for hotels. Addendum 13 is an example of a thorough specification. Like all FF&E items, casegoods are put out to bid; therefore, it is imperative that everyone is bidding on the same specifications. Below is a list of items that should be considered when specifying casegoods.

1. Type of furniture and drawer space is determined by the type of property. A high trafficked, transient business hotel with an average stay of 2 days, does not warrant an overabundance of closet or drawer space. On the other hand, a hotel that caters heavily to groups and families with a longer than average night stay, would warrant a larger percentage of D/D rooms, (double/double—rooms occupied by 2 or more and have two full size beds), and this tells the designer that more clothing storage space is needed.

2. Drawers—Hotel patrons use them to hang clothes on, prop up their feet, use as a stool and are opened and closed with force . . . often. It is imperative that proper glides and supports are noted. Drawers that are supported on both sides, as opposed to one down the center, offer more support but can be more expensive. It may be more cost effective to specify more expensive hardware, thus limiting your maintenance expenses.

3. The actual layout of the casegoods in the guestroom will help you determine which pieces will have to be fully finished on all sides. Often, when a piece will always be flush against the wall, it is not uncommon for a designer to specify an "unfinished back". It is a cost savings, but you will have no flexibility should your layout be altered. This is rarely the case when specifying an armoire or credenza, as your layout options in standard guestrooms are very minimal and would not warrant a "floating" piece of furniture this size.

4. Hardware—If hardware is being used (as opposed to a touch latch or a built-in contour type of handle), it is important to review the style, type of finish, how it will be applied to the drawer front, and availability in case replacement is required. Also, can it support the weight and size of the drawer? Is it mounted flush as to avoid snagging a patrons clothing? Will it tarnish if used in a tropical setting? Will it be difficult to repair?

5. How is the inside of the piece finished? Laminate? Waterproof? Vinylcoating? Finished Wood? Exposed hardware? These are all questions one should ask the manufacturer for clarification.

6. If you are writing specifications for casegoods, be sure to include brand names and numbers for shelf brackets and standards, tracks, hinges, pulls, and drawer slides. This information is usually furnished by the manufacturer.

7. Careful consideration should be given to all casegoods, and seating for commercial interiors. Always review an actual sample prior to making your final selection, and most certainly before ordering 200 rooms of it!

As you go through all of your specifications in the guestroom, it is imperative to continually refer back on your "objective notes". These would be notes from your meetings with the client, your feasibility study, and/or your corporate specifications . . . things such as TV size, accommodations for a VCR shelf, minibar, interior light for the armoire, built-in radio in nightstand, pencil drawer on desk, etc. Once you have determined what pieces will be needed in your guestroom, their style and specific needs, move forward and fit your casegoods and chairs into the existing floor plan. If you are not going with custom casegoods, and are using standard FF&E items, make certain they fit into your layout. Remember when doing an initial layout, you were using generic sizes. Be certain that at all times, your drawings are current on all changes.

Seating

In our standard guestroom (Refer to Add. 4), we have two desk chairs and one comfortable chair. Because the desk chairs are also used for dining, and the restraints of the room, it is necessary to specify armless chairs, so that they may be tucked under the desk when not in use. In a heavily trafficked hotel, arm chairs can be a real problem. The wood gets nicked and the upholstery soiled. Often, guests will use the arm as the seat, which results in continual breakage. (It does nothing for the hotel's insurance liability either!) The type of guestroom will help you in your choice of specifications for a desk chair. Perhaps a lower to mid-priced hotel might prefer an overall wood frame with a wood or upholstered panel insert on seat back, while a high-end hotel may warrant the look of a fully upholstered desk chair. Obviously, the type of fabric you specify, further determines the look—vinyl vs. nylon vs. tapestry, (low–medium–high-end).

It is imperative that you educate your self in specifying a chair that offers adequate support, firmness, cross bracing between the legs, glides or castors (if applicable), as well as meeting local and state fire codes. The second chair in our layout is a fully upholstered chair with a tight seat back, and reversible cushion seat. A **tight seat back** (one that is permanently stitched or secured to the back of the chair), makes a lot of sense, as no additional plumping or straightening of the pillows is needed by the staff. A reversible cushion has both "pros and cons". The "pro" side is that when the cushion gets soiled, it can be flipped, prolonging the life of the upholstery. The "con" side is that the guest can take it off the chair and use it on the floor, it can be taken on the balcony and perhaps left there in inclement weather, or it can fit in a suitcase and be gone forever! Again, simple items like this should be dealt with in your initial objectives meeting with the client. When specifying seating (Refer to Add. 5), make note of the different heights of seats used for lounging, dining, and working. Also, make sure there is adequate space when the chair is fully extended in your layout. Furniture that is cramped in a guestroom, results in damaged wallcoverings, nicked furniture, and an overall congested room. If an ottoman is part of your room layout, I highly recommend casters for flexibility when using it as an additional seat or when it will be moved around by Housekeeping during the cleaning process.

If connector doors are near your chair placement, you may want to also consider casters on the chair. Dragging a heavy chair across carpet can only damage the chair, as well as the floor surface.

If a sofa or love seat is part of your guestroom package, review the same elements as you would for the chair specifications, and add the following:

- Will this item be used just for seating purposes, or is a sofa bed necessary?
- Verify all clearances if item will be used as a sofa bed
- In the case of a sofa bed, it is strongly recommended that you request a sample piece in order to review the difficulty in setting it up, taking it down, the comfort level, and how it "sits" when used as a sofa. If the piece does not sleep or sit well, it becomes a continual nuisance to the guest, as well as the staff, who has to listen to the complaints.

Refer to Addendum 13 to review complete and well researched specifications that demand both longevity and comfort.

At this point we have covered casegood and softgood items and their relationship to textiles. One of the most important textiles used in the guestroom is the upholstery fabric. While each guestroom type varies, in most layouts there is some sort of seating in the room such as a desk chair, occasional chair, ottoman, bench or sofa.

The specification of the upholstery fabric is critical to the design. Not only for reasons of longevity but, depending on what type of seating is involved in the room, it will dictate how strong of an impact that fabric/pattern will play in the room. A love seat with matching side chairs in the same fabric, is going to play a much more visible part in the design of the guestroom, compared to two wood desk chairs with upholstered seats. A few helpful hints to help guard against overpowering the total scheme with upholstered furniture, are as follows:

1. If there is *minimal* seating in the room, the options are quite easy.
    a. You can be more flexible with textured fabrics as well as prints that coordinate with any major pattern in the room, such as the bedspread.
    b. "Simple" is an easy solution. Select a complimentary color in the scheme and repeat the solid color upholstery fabric on the seating.
    c. Textured fabrics that offer a nice blend of the existing colors also work well.
    d. Stay away from large prints, especially if your seat area is smaller than the repeat in the pattern.
    e. Small prints work well if they are coordinated with other patterns and colors in the room. Avoid patterns that look too busy.

f. When selecting sharp contrasting colors—be careful! Only a highly experienced designer can pull this off effectively.

2. When selecting upholstery fabrics for larger pieces of furniture (i.e. sofa, loveseat, or oversized upholstered chair) in your guestrooms, note the following:
   a. Be very cautious when using large, bold prints.
   b. One suggested way to use large print fabrics is when they will match the fabric used for the bedspread.
   c. Another idea is to use a neutral fabric on the bedspread and use your bold print on the sofa and cornice in the room.
   d. In all cases, prior to making your final selection, request a full yard or at least a memo sample that represents the entire repeat.

Once the type of pattern is determined, the next and probably most important issue, is knowing that your pattern is printed or woven on a durable ground.

While 100% warped cotton sateen, polished cottons and chintzes have a great look, and one is tempted to use them for their large flowing prints in upholstery applications, they are best used when specified for low traffic areas and residential locations. High-end suites are another area these "specialty" upholstery fabrics could be specified. In most cases, the suite is occupied by a discriminating guest, the cost per night of the room is higher, and the room will be refurbished more frequently than a standard guestroom.

Cotton prints are also heavily used in tropical climates. Many times the designer will try to achieve a "look" with these fabrics versus choosing them primarily for longevity purposes. Due to the sun's damaging effects on fabrics, the renovating cycle is more frequent in tropical areas.

If the guestroom is not on a short renovation cycle and is not located in a tropical climate, other long lasting upholstery fabrics could be used. Among these are, woven cottons blended with rayon, silk or ramie. Wool is an excellent choice, but not always affordable, due to it's inflated costs.

Below is a list of fabrics and their characteristics that may have use in a hospitality setting.

Fabrics for Guestroom Use

Antique Satin Satin fabric with slub filling yarns prominent on dull side.

Batiste Lightweight, sheer, plain weave, soft fabric. Made of cotton or polyester blend.

Broadcloth Lightweight, sheer, plain weave, tightly woven, thin yarn fabric with slight crosswise rib. Made of cotton or wool blend.

Brocade Heavy, luxurious fabric with slightly raised Jacquard design.

Calico Lightweight, plain weave, cotton-type fabric usually with bright, small print design on contrasting background.

Canvas Heavy, plain weave, cotton-type, durable fabric.

Chambray Lightweight, plain weave, cotton-type fabric usually with colored warp and white filling yarns.

Chintz Light/medium weight, plain weave, closely woven, fine cotton-type fabric with a glazed (polished) finish.

Damask Heavy, bright, reversible, fine yarn fabric with jacquard design.

Duck Medium to heavyweight, plain weave, durable cotton-type fabric. Slightly lighter than canvas, but heavier than sailcloth.

Foulard A lightweight, filament yarn, twill weave fabric with a soft hand. Frequently printed with small overall design (foulard print).

Gauze Very light, sheer, open construction, plain weave, cotton-type fabric.

Matelasse Medium/heavyweight, luxurious, double cloth fabric with a blistered or quilted surface.

Moire Taffeta Tafetta with moire or watermark design.

Muslin Light to medium weight, plain weave, stiff, unfinished cotton fabric with speckled effect from the "trash" content (i.e., foreign matter such as twigs, leaves, etc.)

Ninon Lightweight, plain weave, sheer, open construction fabric with high twist filament yarns giving the fabric a crisp hand.

Sailcloth Medium to heavyweight, plain weave, durable, cotton-type fabric.

Sateen Medium weight, cotton-type fabric with satin weave and semi-lustrous surface.

Satin Medium weight fabric with filament yarns. Satin weave and fine closely woven warp yarns.

Shantung Medium weight, plain weave, silk-like fabric with pronounced **slub** yarns.

Tapestry Heavy, spun yarn, ribbed fabric with colored jacquard design resulting from different colored groupings of warp yarns (visible on fabric back).

Ticking Heavy, strong, closely woven, cotton-type fabric, usually made with stripes or woven designs.

Velour Medium weight, cotton-type, dense, cut pile fabric that resembles velvet.

Velvet Medium weight, synthetic or silk filament yarn fabric with cut pile surface which "stands erect".

Voile Lightweight, sheer, crisp, plain weave, hight twist spun yarns, cotton-type fabric with very, very fine yarns.

Lighting

There are three types of lighting used in the majority of all standard guestrooms.

1. Hardwire Fixture
Located directly into a **j-box** (junction box), in the ceiling or wall.

2. Decorative Fixture
Free standing decorative lighting includes lamps and torcheres.

3. Wallmount Lamp
A fixture that is secured directly to the wall, but is plugged into the wall via a cord, and is not a permanent mount.

Hardwire

Hardwire fixtures are usually specified as entry lights, mounted tight to the ceiling and centered in the entry area. The size of the entry determines the wattage you should specify. A clear glass fixture with 60 watts is normally adequate. If you are unsure of the requirements, consult the lighting engineer or consultant on the project, to verify proper wattage. This fixture is usually operated by a switch inside the door entrance.

In some cases, a hardwire chandelier or pendant type fixture is ceiling mounted over a dining table if one is part of the guestroom package.

Again, let me repeat that these are only rules of thumb for standard guestrooms, and do not necessarily apply to all applications. The bathroom can also offer a hardwire decorative fixture near the vanity or the mirror.

Decorative

Lamps of all materials such as glass, metal, brass, ceramic, crystal, etc. are all available to the hotel designer. Choosing a material that compliments and defines your accents, is an important one. Style, color, and height are all factors that should be considered.

Lamps used on the nightstands should be tall enough (28–32'' preferably), to spread adequate light for reading and illuminating the nightstand itself. Lamps used on a desk should offer adequate lighting to work by, as well as adding to the total light available in the space.

When considering lamps on the dresser space, it is imperative you have space available for it. A cluttered dresser top that houses a TV, ice bucket, marketing literature, room service menus, etc., can leave very little space for a lamp. A wallmount fixture is an option to the dresser lamp and the nightstand lamp, in that both areas are "confined" spaces.

Wallmount

Wallmount fixtures have become increasingly popular in the mid to late 80's. Why? They are extremely versatile. They can be secured at any height, they can have extensions for flexibility, the cord can be concealed with a coordinating cord cover, and they offer easy installation.

In all cases, when specifying lighting for guestrooms, review the following checklist to insure a complete and well researched specification:

- Cord lengths need to reach outlets.

- Color of cord should be specified, especially if it is visible in the room. It should blend in with the background. Clear works well in most areas.

- Is the lamp to be secured to the furniture surface? If so, specify appropriate hardware.

- A 3-way light vs. a single—review with client for preference.

- Shades should match or at least coordinate.

- Specify the location of lamp's on/off switch. Usually when deviating from the catalog specification, there will be an extra add-on charge.

- Request actual finish samples, as catalogs can be deceiving.

In all cases, make sure your total wattage is reviewed and approved by a lighting specialist to insure adequate lighting.

Accessories

The finale of any design is putting the finishing touches to your guestroom design. Hopefully when you get to this point, there are still available dollars for your artwork in the budget.

Again, refer to your "owner objective" notes or "corporate specifications" notes, and these may help you determine how many pieces, possibly the location, and perhaps even the subject matter of the artwork itself. At any rate, your color palette is already complete, therefore, this is the spectrum of colors in which to produce artwork that will tie in with the existing scheme and accents the way artwork should. Items to consider when specifying artwork are: the artwork medium, the subject, should they be safety secured, matting, frame style, size, budget, etc., should all be determined before your research begins. If you are working with a variety of manufacturers, send them each a list of objectives, along with swatches of your fabrics, so that they can submit actual artwork samples, along with matt samples and frames, that will coordinate with your scheme. It is wise to pay close attention to your security mechanism if that is a priority in your objectives. It is important that the completed artwork reflect the room. In a tropical design, perhaps you could have tropical blooms as a subject matter, and in a traditional design, you might consider a still life subject. Do not limit yourself to one source. Artwork is the finishing touch to any room, so take the time to secure pieces that enhance your design.

In standard guestroom design, with the exception of the wood framed mirror that will match the casegoods, artwork is the only accessory. In high-end hotels, you may find silk flowers arranged to adorn tables or floor plants. Again, before ordering either in quantity, request a "finished" piece to be viewed before making your final selections. Be certain that in the case of silk arrangements, the vases are weighted properly, and all stems are individually glued and secured to the inside of the container, so that it remains intact and attractive. To insure that all specified artwork is properly hung in its designated location, elevation drawings will be necessary. These drawings serve several purposes. First, they will allow you to judge the scale of the piece of artwork, in conjunction with the furnishings that will surround it. The size and shape of the artwork will also determine at what floor height the piece will be hung, and these heights should not always be the same. In order to insure proper viewing of your selected pieces, a standard eye level anywhere between 4' and 5' ft. is generally used. The actual arrangement of the artwork on the walls will sometimes vary as well, depending on the type of guestroom or suite you are designing. Rarely in commercial design, will you see stagger or stack art groupings. Typical hotel guestrooms commonly use what are known as **dypticks** (2 matching or coordinating pieces side by side), or **trypticks** (3 matching or coordinating pieces side by side). In either arrangement each piece is placed side by side and spaced 4″ or less from frame to frame. When designing more lavish suites that often have that "residential" feel, the designer may choose a more relaxed or unique approach for groupings of art. Refer to Addendum 6 for an example of an elevation drawing that clearly depicts the location of the artwork over the headboard. Note the **A.F.F.** measurement (Above Finished Floor). This measurement signifies that the A.F.F. measurement of 4′3″ is where the bottom of the frame should be installed. On the bottom of the drawing a 6′ measurement from the wall to the center of the artwork designates the final measurement needed for determining the actual installation location.

In all cases, no matter how accurate the drawings are, it is best to install the artwork and other wall mounted items in the "sample room" to verify your locations, prior to allowing the installation crew to hang all items as per drawings.

These elevation drawings are also very useful in pursuing installation bids, as well as providing an overall review of the look and the placement of items in the guestroom.

Chapter 3 Quiz

1. Choosing from fabrics conducive to Hospitality use, select three bedspread fabrics, each with a coordinating or matching drapery fabric and critique in order, which one would work the best in the guestroom and why.

2. Using four different sized windows in your home, do a drawing and provide the following information on each window:

   A. Finished size of draperies.

   B. Determine what the stack back will be for each window size.

3. Select three different types of carpet and complete specification sheets on each. On paper, critique in order which carpet would work best in the guestroom and why.

4. Select one style of hotel guestroom furniture and design an armoire to match your specification. The armoire must include a mini-bar refrigerator and TV with VCR shelf.

Guestroom Bath Specifications

As a rule, standard guestroom baths are a very compact and efficient use of space. The hotel with whom you are contracted will dictate the "standards" for your bath.

A generic guestroom bath consists of a water closet, a tub or tub enclosure, shower (either separate or included in bathtub), single sink with vanity and mirror, overhead lighting and heat lamp. You are more apt to install separate shower stalls, bidets, double sinks and spas in suites or high-end hotels.

Flooring and Wall Surfaces

Beginning with the floor surface, it is imperative to first find out the recommended spec of the Owner and/or Franchise. A 2″ × 2″ tile that offers a slip-resistant finish is the generic standard for today's mid-priced hotel guestrooms. Two of the major factors to keep in mind when specifying floor tile are:

1. Select a neutral color rather than the current vogue. Color trends come and go, as will the guestroom design, but the floor tile will far outlive the other specifications you are coordinating for the guestroom. Beiges, grays and whites are always acceptable and work well with most schemes. These colors also give a clean, sanitary look which is favored by hotel guests. Another plus is that light colors give the illusion that the room is larger than actual size.

2. Specify a grout that not only complements the tile, but one that will help conceal soil. For example, when using an ecru colored tile you might consider a soft gray grout rather than a pure white. Even the most thorough housekeeping staff would have a difficult time keeping the grout "white". Often times a colored grout is used to accent the wallcovering, paint trim or vanity top. Again, be careful with trendy color schemes. If a color such as mauve were chosen, it might look very nice with the present wallcovering, but it could be a real eyesore when the color mauve is passe'. One exception to using a colored grout would be when matching the color to the vanity top. If pink marble was specified for the vanity top, for example, assume that the top will be there as long as the tile. The pink grout complements the overall scheme quite nicely. The pink toned vanity and grout dictate the scheme in that particular guestroom for the lifetime of those two materials.

   Moving on to the wall treatments for the guestroom baths, one usually has three choices—vinyl, tile or paint, or any combination of three. If a **tub enclosure** (a one-piece, molded unit that includes three walls and the tub) is not being specified, a tile application is most practical to use on the walls surrounding the tub.

Although any size tile can actually be used, it is wise to use a larger tile on the wall than what is on the floor for the following reasons:

1. You have a greater space to cover and the larger scale has a neat, clean appearance.

2. You have less grout lines which will lower your installation costs.

3. You will have less grout lines to crack or soil, requiring less maintenance time.

The tile specified in this area should be a glossy finish. It cleans better, and this is an area where a slip-resistant **coefficient** (codes determining the amount of slip guard on a tile surface) does not apply. When choosing the color of the wall tile and the grout, please keep in mind the basic factors previously discussed concerning the floor tile:

1. Select a color that will not date itself.

2. Select a color that will always have a fresh sanitized look.

3. Select a grout color that will be easily maintained and complement the overall scheme.

What about the remaining walls that are not tiled? If your specification will be wallpaper, remember that you will need a wallcovering that is easy to clean, such as a vinyl coated paper. Be certain that in a small guestroom bath, you specify patterns that are in scale to the size of the space, as well as a pattern that coordinates or complements the wall treatment in the guestroom. Paper wallcoverings are acceptable for use in a high-end suites, as they are refurbished more often and you will find them available in more formal, intricate designs and patterns. This however, does not eliminate the maintenance concerns or soilage you will find evident when using a paper wallcovering. When specifying wallcoverings for the guestroom bath, it is not necessary to specify 54" wide materials, since there are no large areas that require large expanses of the wallcovering. In a confined space such as this, a 27" width is not only standard but more than adequate and much easier to handle.

If painting is specified for the guestroom bath, have a sample area painted for viewing to insure the color meets with your approval. A semi-gloss enamel paint in a light, neutral color is recommended in areas that require continuous cleaning. A white semi-gloss paint is a standard specification for a guestroom bath ceiling; only in the case of a high-end or specialty suite, is wallpaper or colored paint applied to the ceiling.

Many times paint is specified for the wall surface because of budget restraints. In this case you may want to consider using a wallpaper border at the ceiling line (along with the painted wall surface). This technique adds warmth to the bath without adding a lot of additional expense to the space.

Vanity/Tub/Fixtures

The next consideration in the guestroom bath is the vanity. Laminate finishes are sometimes used on hospitality vanities. Presently favored are man-made products resembling marble and natural stones, i.e. cultured marble. **Corian** is viable alternative. It too, is a man-made product that offers the client an even more realistic stone look. The mid-to-late 80's took it a step further and produced Avonite and a variety of other stone alternates that offer texture and color. Tile, slate, agglomerate marble, granite, etc. are all additional hard surface materials acceptable for use in bathroom vanities, residential and commercial. It is wise to request a large sample and a manufacturer's presentation of the material you are considering. This allows you to review the material and learn more about it's possible applications and capabilities.

It is recommended that the single sink be placed in the center of the vanity top to provide space on each side of the sink.

Depending on the water closet location, it may be necessary to off-center the sink for good clearance. A china bowl sink, separately hung below the vanity or an integral sink bowl built into a Corian vanity, are both examples of acceptable specifications in today's mid-priced hotel rooms.

Lighting/Misc.

Be certain to include adequate lighting over the vanity areas. A common complaint, especially with women travelers, is that there is rarely good light in hotel baths for applying cosmetics. The two most common light treatments you will see over vanities are hard wire decorative light fixtures, or an overhead soffit with **parabolic lenses.** The latter of these methods is not only cost effective, but produces ample light by the use of fluorescent bulbs, providing a proper parabolic lense is used to direct the light downward. Another source of light in the hotel guestroom bath is the standard heatlamp. Should there be a separate shower stall in the bath, it should be equipped with an interior downlight in it.

Another important aspect of designing the guestroom bath is to provide sufficient electrical outlets at the correct height. If wall mounted hair dryers are being specified as part of the amenity package, be certain to allow an extra outlet for that appliance. In most cases the standard guestroom bath offers one duplex outlet, at the vanity height.

Other items to include on your elevation drawings are:

1. Towel bars
2. Toilet paper dispenser
3. Kleenex dispenser
4. Detractable clothes line
5. Shower curtain rod
6. Height of shower nozzle
7. Cloths hook on back of door
8. Mirror over vanity
9. Phone location

It is imperative to check for "corporate standard" specifications when dealing with these items, as some standards will define specific locations or determine their necessity at all.

Chapter 4 Quiz

1. A. Research various materials that can be utilized for bath vanities. Choose three sources and present information on each.

    B. Make a recommendation on which would be the most suitable specification for your job.

2. Using Addendum 3 (1/4" scale) as a reference, elevate each of the bath walls as you would design it.
    A. Locate bath accessories, such as towel bars, mirror, etc.

3. Draw an electrical plan for the bath in Addendum 3.

4. Compile all materials for a colorboard for your guestroom bath.

Chapter Five

Guestroom Corridors

The **corridor** is a hallway, arcade, passageway, or gallery that joins the guestrooms to any wing of the hotel. Corridors may be interior (no outdoor exposure) or exterior (with outdoor exposure). In either case, they are extensions of your public spaces and guestrooms, and they require very special design considerations to insure that the design theme and color palette will have a continuous flow.

In Chapter 5 we will discuss each of the following areas to consider when designing corridors:

1. Flooring
2. Wallcovering
3. Lighting
4. Signage
5. Elevator Lobbies
6. Accessories

Flooring

The first and most critical part of the corridor design is specifying the floor surface. Some standard specifications for commercial carpet are axminster, nylon or printed broadloom. Patterns and small prints can be specified and coordinated with the style and design of the hotel.

A palm leaf design used in a tropical resort would be a good example. Although it is rare to find a solid colored carpet in a hotel corridor, a solid carpet may be used as a coordinating border.

Whatever the carpet application, it is most important that the design, color and pattern are a continuous flow from the hotel's public spaces through the guestrooms. The carpet pattern can be continuous or broken up by using a series of insets, framed by borders. If a border or inset look is preferred, it is imperative that a carpet drawing be completed (see Addendum 18), which specifies the appropriate widths of the carpet and shows the treatment of the corners and elevator lobbies. It is suggested to use as few seams as possible when designing your layout, because of the daily use of housekeeping carts and luggage racks. Remember that all corridors are not straight. They can curve, turn, inset and offset at doorways. Using these to your advantage, very interesting results may be achieved when using a border carpet or pattern.

In many corridors, there are sections that may be glass windows. These may be window-wall sections or completely enclosed glass structures used as bridges between guestroom wings.

In either case, you may consider changing your flooring specification in these areas, so that they are less likely to fade from direct sun exposure. A good low-maintenance alternate would be a non-skid tile, color-coordinated and butted on both sides to your carpet. A hard surface specification is also recommended for entry ways and vending areas.

Wallcovering

Specifications in wall surfaces for corridors may vary from vinyl wallcoverings to paint, depending on the particular style and design of the hotel. As an example, a neutral or colored stucco wallcovering or paint finish would be appropriate in a Mediterranean style hotel.

In most mid-to-high-end hotels, an 18 ounce or higher weight vinyl wallcovering is standard for interior corridors. Due to the large expanse of wall space, a 54" wallcovering is the recommended specification. It will require less seaming and lower installation costs as opposed to 27" goods.

Review the chart on the next page when specifying wall vinyls to determine what class type should be used for your application, taking into consideration, light exposure, traffic patterns and the intended life cycle required for the material.

Lighting

Lighting is an extremely important aspect of interior corridors, as little or no natural light is available. Your wallcovering and carpet should be specified first for this area, and their colors will dictate how much light will be required in the corridor. A very dark carpet will absorb more of the light than a soft pastel color. This same theory applies to the wallcovering hues.

Decorative wall sconces, directly mounted (hardwire) are the most prevalent main source of light in corridors. Other sources of light may be from recessed cans or strip lighting used in conjunction with parabolic lenses. The strip lighting/parabolic lense combination is often used when entry guestroom doors are recessed, in order to illuminate the entry door numbers and improve visibility to the key lock. Certain wall sconces will also illuminate both ceiling and wall, and these are primarily used when a ceiling has decorative architectural features.

When specifying wall sconces, it is recommended to choose a fully enclosed fixture, rather than one with an exposed bulb. It is possible that debris may be put in the fixture, thus causing a hazardous condition.

Also, when specifying your fixture, consider that these may be items that are overlooked by housekeeping, therefore they may not be cleaned or polished on a daily basis. Finishes such as frosted glass vs. clear glass, brushed brass vs. polished, etc. will be easier to maintain a clean and crisp look.

When designing a new construction hotel, the height of the fixture on the wall is very important. Ceiling height can vary from hotel to hotel and the fixture location is determined by the height of the ceiling. The taller the ceiling, the higher the fixture is mounted for an even spread of light. The average mounted height for corridor fixtures is 5–5 1/2 ft. The finished height will ultimately depend on the style of the fixture and where the mounting bracket is

WALLCOVERING STANDARDS

	Class I	Class II	Class III	Class IV	Class V	Class VI
	Decorative	Decorative and Serviceable	Decorative with good service ability	Decorative with full service ability	Medium commercial serviceability	Full commercial serviceability
Minimum colorfastness		23 hours	46 hours	46 hours	200 hours	200 hours
Minimum washability		100 cycles	100 cycles	100 cycles	100 cycles	100 cycles
Minimum scrubbability			50 cycles	200 cycles	300 cycles	500 cycles
Minimum abrasion resistance			500 cycles	1000 cycles	300 cycles	1000 cycles
Minimum breaking strength			(#8 Greige duck) 20 lb (89N)	(#8 Greige duck) 30 lb (133N)	(#0 Emery paper) 55 lb (245N)	(#0 Emery paper) 951 lb (423N)
Minimum crocking resistance			10 cycles	10 cycles	20 cycles	20 cycles
Minimum stain resistance			Reagents 1–9	Reagents 1–12	Reagents 1–12	Reagents 1–12
Minimum tear resistance				5-point scale (w/o weight)	25-point scale (with weight)	50-point scale (with weight)
Maximum blocking resistance					2-point scale	2-point scale
Minimum coating adhesion					6-lb/2-in. strip (27-N/5-cm strip)	6-lb/2-in. strip (27-N/5-cm strip)
Minimum cold cracking resistance					Pass	Pass
Minimum heat aging resistance					Pass	Pass
Minimum shrinkage					2.5%	2.5%

Source: The Chemical Fabrics and Film Association

located on the back side of the fixture. For example, in a renovation situation where the electrical box is located on the wall, it is important to specify a wall sconce with a low mounting bracket that has the majority of its overall height in the upper half of the fixture, so that it will have the appearance of being hung at the appropriate height.

When specifying a fixture for a corridor, the type of bulb that will be used should be considered carefully. The initial cost of the bulb, the number of foot candles it will give, expected user hours, labor hours for Engineering to replace the bulbs and availability. As an example, a 13 watt **fluorescent** PL lamp radiates approximately the same foot candles as a 60 watt incandescent bulb and lasts almost twice as long.

It is possible you may not be responsible for determining what type of bulb will be used in the fixture, but it is important to be aware of your choices and to consider the needs of the hotel operation team.

As in all interior spaces, it is crucial to have an electrical consultant or engineer review your lighting specifications to verify the appropriate light levels.

Signage

Probably one of the most functional aspects of hotel design is **signage**. There are three kinds of signage in a hotel, directional signage, outlet signage and room number signage. Upon the guest entering the front doors of the hotel, directional signage directs the guest to all public areas of the hotel. Room signage designates individual room numbers. Outlet signage would be the signage designated for the restraurant name, ballroom name etc.

Directional signage is best left to the operations of the hotel for final determination of location and contents. It is suggested that the directional signage match that of the room number signage. Outlet signage would match to specific logos of the outlet.

In all cases, your signage should be easily read and the finishes should coordinate with the materials throughout the hotel. Before committing to an entire order from your signage vendors, be sure to request a sample for final review.

If your project is a guestroom renovation, you will most likely be responsible for room numbers and corridor signage. In most cases, they will match the existing signage throughout the hotel.

If your project is new construction, you will want to consider the following when specifying new signage:

1. Material
2. Type Set
3. Mounting to wall or door
4. Budget

Addendum 19 features a drawing of a custom guestroom door sign, designed for a resort lodge with an Indian motif design throughout the facility. The colors of the hotel's logo were selected from the Pantone Matching System Guide (PMS) and repeated on the top portion of the room number.

Elevator Lobbies/Accessories

If the project you are designing involves elevator lobbies, you have the opportunity to design within the corridor space. Carpet border, decorative benches, mirrors, artwork, upgraded wall sconces, pots and plants all combine to make an inviting entrance/exit area for the guests. The elevator lobbies are special areas and require full elevation drawings to properly locate all specified items.

Chapter 5 Quiz

1. After reviewing Addendum 18, draw a reflected ceiling plan that includes over-head lighting at guestroom entry door. Include sconce lighting locations in an elevation of 18–20 ft. of corridor length.

2. Design a door number sign.

3. Select a carpet/vinyl, wallcovering, elevator lobby furnishings for a corridor design. Compile a color board and complete specification sheets for each selection.

4. Draw a carpet layout for a corridor that includes an elevator lobby. Carpet insets and borders should be inclusive.

Chapter Six

The Process

Specification Book

Thus far, you have been exposed to a comprehensive study of the FE&E specification process, and you are now ready to commit these specifications to paper—namely, the Specification Form. There are many variations of specification forms. Develop one yourself or use one that is in existence and familiar to your client. Condensing your specification information is very important and should be easily understood by everyone involved with the project. See Addendum 14 for different layouts of specification forms.

Following is information that must be included on the Specification Form:

1. Identify product and number
2. Manufacturer
3. Quantity/yardage
4. Measurements
5. Weight (very important when specifying carpet and wallpaper, for example)
6. Location of item
7. Finish if applicable
8. Revisions—date/area
9. Project name

Information of secondary importance:

1. Color scheme
2. Designer who specified item
3. Delivery date expected
4. P.O. number
5. Notation for who supplies and installs (ex.: G.C. supplied)
6. Miscellaneous section for notes

As specifications are changed or items discontinued, a new specification sheet is made up and the original destroyed. Specification books are an essential tool in providing an efficient method for the purchasing agent to use for the bid process. *Incomplete* or *inaccurate* specification sheets cause delays, wrong orders, and waste valuable time. It is the responsibility of the designer to *check* and *recheck* the specification to insure it is correct.

When a specification is sent for bidding, it is necessary that the specification read: "or equal". This means that the bidder can offer a substitution that will meet the bidding requirements and the budget of the client.

When bidding on wallcovering and carpeting, it is important that all quantities carry the notation: "to be verified and **field measured**". This is particularly important when calculations are taken from drawings, as opposed to obtaining final quantities from the installer.

Specification sheets are used in several ways. First, a completed package of specification sheets are sent for project approval, client approval, corporate approval, and even supervisor approval. Secondly, the General Contractor and/or Installer will use it for reference during the installation. The specification book is used repeatedly during this process. It is important to add an actual sample (fabric for example), or a clear picture to identify the specification. When an item is too large or heavy to mount in the specification book, often the designer will instruct the reader to refer to the color board. A good example of this would be ballroom carpet or bathroom tile.

After the project is completed, a specification book continues to offer information, and is filled for future reference. With all of the wear and tear that is common and expected in commercial spaces, it is very easy for the designer, owner or hotel employee to refer to the specification book, should they have to re-order an item to replace an original specification that may be damaged or worn.

Who receives a spec book? This depends on what was negotiated in your design contract. The following parties should be considered when issuing specification books:

- Design firm retains one copy
- Owner/client
- Operator—if applicable
- Hotel staff member, (usually the General Manager, requires that Housekeeping, Engineering, or the Rooms Division staff keep a file on the project.)
- General Contractor
- Purchasing Agent—if applicable
- Project Manager or installer—which ever is applicable
- If the hotel is a franchise, the Corporation may require a copy for approval and for their files.

Sometimes a specification book is issued to whomever is doing the receiving of the FF&E items, although some prefer copies of individual purchase orders to track items.

Remember, a precise, organized specification book is the most important tool in insuring a successful project and the implementation of your design.

Finish Schedule

A finish schedule correlates with the specification book, but it's main function is to dictate the finishes on all walls, floor and ceiling surfaces. A finish schedule is very important to the installer and General Contractor, however a finish schedule for a hotel guestroom contains minimal information and can be incorporated in your specification book. Review Addendum

15 for an abbreviated version of a finish schedule for the guestrooms, as well as a more elaborate schedule used when designing public areas of a new construction hotel.

Color Boards

Early in your specification process, the client will probably require a color board that includes actual samples of fabrics and photographs of furnishings. This board creates a visual textured picture of the completed guestroom. It is critical that this board be layed out so that it clearly displays your specifications as well as "sell" your design. It is not necessary to mount every item, but it is necessary to show items that will impact the design. Carpeting, bedspread, drapery, and wallcovering should be your greatest percentage of coverage and main focal points on the board. Upholstery fabric would occupy a smaller percentage of color board space. A color photo of one or two pieces of your casegoods should be included as well as one lamp style. Do not crowd your board. You are better off using two boards than to clutter one. The client will have a hard time envisioning his guestrooms, and in turn, you will make your "sell" difficult. If your board is organized, neat, and easily read, it will go a long way in showing your efforts and organizational skills to your viewers. Insuring straight matt cuts, firmly glued samples, well wrapped foam core with fabric samples, as well as draped or pleated fabrics on the board, will enhance the overall look.

These boards will be used for presentations to the client, and possibly be displayed in the sales office or at the project site. They will be viewed, shipped and handled by many throughout the project, deeming it imperative that it be assembled correctly, as it is a true reflection of you and your organization. Refer to Addendum 16 for an example of a color board layout.

As you review this color board sample, please note the following:

- The largest sample on the board is the bedspread. The print design, color and pattern make it the main focus of the room.

- The next dominate sample is the wallcovering. Though it may be a non-descript, textured vinyl, when it covers the entire perimeter of the room, it will produce a major impact on the color palette of the room.

- The next largest sample is the carpet, as it will occupy the entire floor surface, with the exception of the bathroom floor.

- The drapery sample is small. It may require a bigger sample if it has a large repeat.

- Please note that not *every* casegood sample needs to be shown on your board. It is important that several pieces be shown to reflect the style of furniture used.

- The size of upholstery fabric swatches are determined in accordance with what they will be covering. The fabric used for a sofa would be considered more of a focal point than that of a chair.

It is also beneficial to number samples so that during your presentation you can easily reference it's location to the client. A "key" and layout (as shown on Addendum 16–page 3) are placed on the back-side of the color board for easy reference.

The way in which your color boards are finished is very important. The use of coordinating matts, framing the board with wood or metal or bordering your boards with black electrical tape, the use of project titles, or adding your company logo, will play an important role in a thoroughly well designed guestroom presentation. Several alternatives are shown for your review in Addendum 16.

If you are not able to obtain color photographs of the casegoods for example, you may want to add a quarter-inch matt border around the black & white photograph to enhance and coordinate with the remaining samples on the board. Review Addendum 16, Page 2, for sample layouts and matt finishes. Colorboard I reflects a full matt presentation, while Colorboard II has a "window" effect, where all items are mounted on the baseboard and a coordinating matt is cut and mounted on the top of the baseboard. The "window" type colorboard is a more difficult approach, but it has a very unique effect. Last, support your boards with foamcore for stability and be creative!

Renderings

A **rendering** is a perspective drawing depicting a designer's conception of a finished room or space. Usually completed by a skilled artist who specializes in this type of drawing, renderings can be of various mediums such as charcoal, pencil, ink, watercolor etc.

When a client requests a rendering it is wise to negotiate this as an addition to the design contract as costs may widely vary on renderings depending on the size, the detail involved and the medium chosen. Further costs are incurred when the rendering is sub-contracted out to an artist as opposed to using an on-staff artist.

Many times it is difficult for the designer to negotiate rendering costs to a client even though it gives the client a clear depiction of what the final product will be. The advantage of the rendering to the designer is that the drawing is a very useful tool in selling your design.

Addendum 20, page 1, offers a generic rendering using dimensional "block" furniture. This type of drawing will give the client a feel for the layout of the room. Addendum 20, page 2, takes this drawing a step further and adds detailed characteristics to the FF&E specifications. In the 3rd and 4th drawings of Addendum 20, an isometric view is offered in both block and detailed stages. This is another type of perspective drawing commonly used in renderings. As a final finish to your drawing, wash with color and mount to add yet another exciting dimension to your drawing. Practice both of these techniques for future use, using the grid provided.

Presentation

After the specs, finish schedule and color boards are complete, the next process is the presentation. Many times the presentation to the client is carried out by the design firm's owner, Senior Designer or project captain. Regardless of who does it, it is imperative that *they know their products!* Another piece that will be well utilized is a layout of the guestroom, which is black lined and slightly washed with color, and again mounted for the presenter to use as a reference when reviewing the various specifications.

In the guestroom that has special detailing of a window treatment, wet bar, etc. It would be appropriate to have a mounted elevation available also.

A few guidelines to insure a successful presentation are as follows:

1. Presenter should be in appropriate business attire. You should be aware of the color selections on your boards, and coordinate your attire accordingly. Be aware of color and pat-

terns in your attire; you don't want to be in competition with your color boards and detract from your presentation. The *color boards* are the *focal point.*

2. Good posture, adequate eye contact, and a firm handshake are always appropriate in an initial meeting and presentation.

3. Be sure to introduce yourself, your company, and state the objectives you worked with in producing the design . . . then move right into the color board presentation.

4. Speak clearly and don't get too wordy. For example, *Correct:* "A 100% nylon, 32 ounce, cutpile carpet is being used in all guestrooms". (Point to sample board.) *Incorrect:* "A 100% nylon Monsanto with jute back, tufted and twisted yarns, comes in 12 ft. widths, is being used in all guestrooms". As you can see, while the 2nd presentation of the carpet is very informative, the 1st presentation is more than adequate for the client.

   It is important however, for the presenter to know the additional information on the carpet or at least have a specification book at hand for easy reference, should the client ask additional questions. There is no reason to challenge your memory, or clutter the mind of the client, who only wants to know if the product is of quality and looks good.

5. It is very helpful to have on hand larger pieces of fabric, wallcovering and carpet (especially in the case of large pattern repeats), to allow the client to view and touch. Once they are glued to the board, it is difficult to critique. If artwork is being used in the guestroom, it is best to have an actual sample for the client to view.

6. If the client is not responding favorably to a certain specification, try to find out what he dislikes about it, and offer other suggestions. If further research and selections are needed, set a date as to meet and discuss alternates. You should be prepared to offer your reasoning behind your spec, but do not attempt to defend or deny the issue. The client may have specific ideas about the project and you could lose your client. Hopefully, these issues were covered at the onset of the project when objectives were discussed, but he has a right to change his mind.

7. If, for some reason you do not have an answer, do not offer a temporary or incorrect one to pacify the customer. Let him know you would like to check your sources, refer back to your notes, etc., then get back to him the next day with an answer. *Do not* jeopardize the confidence your client has in you with an incorrect answer. Prompt follow up is critical.

8. Upon completion of the presentation, always inquire if there are any questions. Confirm any items that require additional research and the time when you will get back to them, and of course, thank them for their time and attention.

Handle the appropriate follow up as necessary. *Don't* drop the ball or delegate and forget about it. In the clients eyes, you as the presenter of the design, are in charge and responsible. Strong, thorough and professional presentations can make or break any design review. Having followed the client's objectives and having fully researched all the of FF&E specifications, should give you the confidence to produce a successful presentation.

Chapter 6 Quiz

1. After reviewing the suggested specification sheets on Addendum 14, develop a specification sheet of your own. Write a synopsis explaining why this type of form would work for both client and designer.

2. Develop a specification book for the bath you designed in Chapter 4.

3. Using the Finish Schedule in Addendum 15, complete the schedule in accordance with the guestroom you designed in Chapter 3.

4. Using the layout of your choice in Addendum 17, render a guestroom in either of the techniques depicted in Addendum 20.

5. Based on the color board you have completed. Do an oral presention on your design.

Appendixes

The 1990's have brought about tremendous change to our traditional and standard guestrooms and the number of hotel franchises available.

A brief explanation of the different types of hotels along with several examples of guestroom layouts are available in Addendum 17.

A. Full Service Hotel

A **full service** hotel offers a selection of guestroom types, food and beverage facilities, meeting/banquet facilities, usually a pool and/or health club facilities, public spaces such as Lobby, Lobby Lounge and many times upgraded club or concierge floors and retail space. Examples of full service hotels are Marriott, Westin, Omni & Hyatt.

B. Limited Service Hotel

A **limited service** hotel offers many guestroom conveniences, but lack in amenities with minimal or no restaurant/lounge, meeting or retail facilities. This concept is many times referred to as "Suite Concept".

The guestrooms are slightly larger, sometimes divided into two separate areas as in living room and sleeping areas. Amenities such as mini refrigerator, microwave and VCR are sometimes available. This concept is very popular as the rates are usually less than full service hotels and some offer all inclusive complimentary breakfast and a limited, complimentary Happy Hour. Examples of limited service or suite concepts are Quality Inn, Radisson, Embassy Suites and Marriott Courtyards.

In Addendum 17, a variety of layouts are provided for easy reference. As new concepts develop, layouts change and old ones are deleted. These are some of the most popular layouts of the 1990's.

VINYL BLACKOUT

ALL VINYL MUST BE INSPECTED OVER LIGHTS FOR ANY DEFECTS BEFORE CUTTING.

DRAPERIES TO BE CUSTOM TABLED FOR EXACT SIZE. ALL SELVAGE TO BE REMOVED. FABRIC TO BE PLEATED ON WHITE FACE, COLOR TO OUTSIDE OF WINDOWS.

SEAMS: French seams to be hidden behind pleats at headings using #25 monofilament thread on vinyl blackout. Using "Lights' out" fabric use 100% polyester thread.

HEADINGS: Permanent finish buckram, four (4) inches deep, fabric self-faced for continuous color appearance on outside and inside, using 100% polyester thread.

BOTTOM HEMS: Double fold four (4) inch self-faced straight stitched bottom hems with sewn closures at overlaps and returns, using #25 monofilament thread on vinyl blackout. Using "Lights out" fabric use 100% polyester thread. No piecing of goods permitted.

SIDE HEMS: Double fold reversed 1–1/2" self-faced straight stitched hems, using #25 monofilament thread on vinyl blackout. Using "Lights out" fabric use 100% polyester thread. No piecing of goods permitted.

WEIGHTS: One inch (1") covered lead weights tacked hem line on each seam and each end.

PLEATS: Triple fold French pleats machine sewn with lock stitch with 14 thread bar or "L" tack one-half (1/2) inch up from bottom of buckram, using #25 monofilament thread on vinyl blackout. Using "Lights out" fabric use 100% polyester thread.

OVERLAPS: Three and one-half (3–1/2) inch with double fold back of buckram.

RETURNS: Three (3) inch with double fold back of buckram.

HOOKS: Pin on Kirsch #1012–C, Stainless Steel.

SLANT TOPS: IF SPECIFIED, ALL SLANT TOPS TO CONFORM TO THE ANGLE OF THE WINDOW AND ALL PLEATS TO BE UPRIGHT. ALL BOTTOM HEMS TO BE LEVEL.

ALL SEWING TO BE DONE USING #25 MONOFILAMENT WHERE APPLICABLE, HIGH HEAT THREAD, CLEAR OR COLOR TO MATCH FABRIC. BOBBIN THREAD IN "L" TACK PROCESS TO USE WHITE COTTON THREAD.

DRAPERY TO BE FAN-FOLDED COMPLETELY DRESSED DOWN WHEN INSTALLED.

Marriott corporation INTERNATIONAL HEADQUARTERS MARRIOTT DRIVE WASHINGTON, D.C. 20058	SHEET TITLE VINYL BLACKOUT SPECIFICATIONS	DATE 8/12/88	DWG NO. 1 of 1

Taken from The Marriott Corporation 189 Generation Casegoods and Softgoods Manual, August, 1988. Reprinted with permission

OPEN-WEAVE CASEMENTS

ALL GOODS MUST BE INSPECTED FOR DEFECTS BEFORE CUTTING.

DRAPERIES TO BE CUSTOM TABLED FOR EXACT SIZE. PARTIAL SELVAGE TO BE REMOVED DEPENDING ON WEAVE OF FABRIC. ALL PATTERNS MUST BE MATCHED.

SEAMS: Overlocked and merrowed seams (serged with a back-up), all seams to be hidden at side of pleat, using 100% polyester thread. French seams might be necessary depending on weave of fabric.

HEADINGS: Double fold four (4) inch with permanent finished buckram, double fold buckram at overlaps and returns, sewn closures, using #25 monofilament thread.

BOTTOM HEMS: Double fold four (4) inch straight stitched. Sewn closures at overlaps and returns, using 100% polyester thread. Lobby and suites to be blindstitched if possible.

SIDE HEMS: Double fold one and one-half (1–1/2) inch blind stitched, using 100% polyester thread.

WEIGHTS: One (1) inch vinyl covered lead weights tacked hem line on each seam and corner.

PLEATS: Triple fold French pleats machine sewn with 14 thread bar, or "L" or "F" tack one-half (1/2) inch up from bottom of buckram, using 100% polyester thread.

OVERLAPS: Three and one-half (3–1/2) inch with double fold back of buckram.

RETURNS: Three (3) inch with double fold back of buckram.

HOOKS: Pin on Kirsch #1012–C, Stainless Steel.

SLANT TOPS: IF SPECIFIED, ALL SLANT TOPS TO CONFORM TO THE ANGLE OF THE WINDOW AND ALL PLEATS TO BE UPRIGHT. ALL BOTTOM HEMS TO BE LEVEL.

DRAPERY TO BE PROPERLY DRESSED AND FAN-FOLDED, COMPLETELY DRESSED DOWN WHEN INSTALLED.

	SHEET TITLE	DATE	DWG NO.
Marriott corporation INTERNATIONAL HEADQUARTERS MARRIOTT DRIVE WASHINGTON, D.C. 20058	OPEN WEAVE CASEMENT SPECIFICATIONS	8/12/88	1 of 1

BLACKOUT LINED DRAPERY

ALL VINYL MUST BE INSPECTED OVER LIGHTS FOR ANY DEFECTS BEFORE CUTTING.

DRAPERIES TO BE CUSTOM TABLED FOR EXACT SIZE. ALL SELVAGE TO BE REMOVED. ALL PATTERNS MUST BE MATCHED.

SEAMS: FABRIC: Merrowed using 100% polyester thread.
LINING: 1/2" flat seam using 100% polyester thread or French seam single needle (Note: This requires more yardage than additional labor cost.)

HEADINGS: Buchram to be inserted between face fabric and lining, stitched across top. On overlaps and returns, double fold back of buckram is 12" on each. Lining to extend to top of finished drapery. Stitch both sides of each side at heading. Top is to be "pillow cased."

BOTTOM HEMS: FABRIC: Double fold four (4) inch straight stitched, sewn closures at overlaps and returns, using 100% polyester thread. Suites to be blindstitched using 100% polyester thread.
LINING: Two (2) inch straight stitched, single turn-up, finishing one and one-half (1-1/2") inches above face fabric, using 100% polyester thread.

SIDE HEMS: Blind stitched one and one-half (1-1/2) inch with lining to edge of drapery for blackout purpose, using 100% polyester thread.

WEIGHTS: FABRIC: One (1") inch vinyl covered lead weights tacked hem line on each seam and corner. If weight is tacked in with tacker, tack should not show on exterior.
LINING: None required.

PLEATS: Triple fold French pleats machine sewn with 14 thread bar, "L" tack or "F" tack one-half (1/2) inch up from bottom of buckram, using #25 monofilament thread.

OVERLAPS: Three and one-half (3-1/2) inch with double fold back of buckram.

RETURNS: Three to six (3-6) inch depending on application with double fold back of buckram.

HOOKS: Pin on Kirsch #1012-C, Stainless Steel.

SLANT TOPS: IF SPECIFIED, ALL SLANT TOPS TO CONFORM TO THE ANGLE OF THE WINDOW AND ALL PLEATS TO BE UPRIGHT. ALL BOTTOM HEMS TO BE LEVEL.

DRAPERY TO BE PROPERLY DRESSED AND FAN-FOLDED, COMPLETELY DRESSED DOWN WHEN INSTALLED.

Marriott corporation INTERNATIONAL HEADQUARTERS MARRIOTT DRIVE WASHINGTON, D.C. 20058	SHEET TITLE BLACKOUT LINED DRAPERY SPECIFICATIONS	DATE 8/12/88	DWG NO. 1 of 1

SHEER DRAPERY

ALL GOODS MUST BE INSPECTED FOR DEFECTS BEFORE CUTTING.

DRAPERIES TO BE CUSTOM TABLED FOR EXACT SIZE. ALL SELVAGE TO BE REMOVED. ALL PATTERNS MUST BE MATCHED.

SEAMS: Overlocked and merrowed seams with overlock stitch (serged with a back-up), all seams to be hidden at side of pleat, using 100% polyester thread, size 100, neutral color to match if needed.

HEADINGS: Double fold four (4) inch with permanent finished buchram, double fold back overlaps and returns, sewn closures, 100% polyester thread.

BOTTOM HEMS: Double fold four (4) inch straight stitched. Sewn closures at overlaps and returns, using 100% polyester thread. Lobbies and suites to be blind stitched.

SIDE HEMS: Double fold one and one-half (1–1/2) inch blind stitched, using 100% polyester thread.

WEIGHTS: Weighted tape, Kirsch #1600 or equal for entire length of bottom hem at bottom of drapery or a little higher.

PLEATS: Triple fold French pleats machine sewn with 14 thread bar, "L" tack or "F" tack one-half (1/2) inch up from bottom of buckram, using #25 monofilament thread.

OVERLAPS: Three and one-half (3–1/2) inch with double fold back of buckram.

RETURNS: Three (3) inch with double fold back of buckram.

HOOKS: Pin on Kirsch #1012–C, *Stainless Steel*.

SLANT TOPS: IF SPECIFIED, ALL SLANT TOPS TO CONFORM TO THE ANGLE OF THE WINDOW AND ALL PLEATS TO BE UPRIGHT. ALL BOTTOM HEMS TO BE LEVEL.

DRAPERY TO BE PROPERLY DRESSED AND FAN-FOLDED, COMPLETELY DRESSED DOWN WHEN INSTALLED.

Marriott corporation INTERNATIONAL HEADQUARTERS MARRIOTT DRIVE WASHINGTON, D.C. 20058	SHEET TITLE SHEER DRAPERY SPECIFICATIONS	DATE 8/12/88	DWG NO. 1 of 1

UNLINED DRAPERY

ALL GOODS MUST BE INSPECTED FOR DEFECTS BEFORE CUTTING.

DRAPERIES TO BE CUSTOM TABLED FOR EXACT SIZE. PARTIAL SELVAGE TO BE REMOVED. ALL PATTERNS MUST BE MATCHED.

SEAMS: Overlocked and merrowed seams (serged with a back-up), all seams to be hidden at side of pleat, using 100% polyester thread.

HEADINGS: Double fold four (4) inch with permanent finished buchram. Fold Double Buck at overlaps and returns, sewn closures, using #25 monofilament thread.

BOTTOM HEMS: Double fold four (4) inch straight stitched. Sewn closures at overlaps and returns, using #25 monofilament thread. Lobby and suite to be blindstitched.

SIDE HEMS: Double fold one and one-half (1–1/2) inch blind stitched, using #25 monofilament thread or 100% polyester thread.

WEIGHTS: One (1) inch vinyl covered lead weights tacked hem line on each seam and corner.

PLEATS: Triple fold French pleats machine sewn with 14 thread bar or "L" tack one-half (1/2) inch up from bottom of buckram, using #25 monofilament thread.

OVERLAPS: Three and one-half (3–1/2) inch with double fold back of buckram.

RETURNS: Three to six (3–6) inch depending on application with double fold back of buckram.

HOOKS: Pin on Kirsch #1012–C, Stainless Steel.

SLANT TOPS: IF SPECIFIED, ALL SLANT TOPS TO CONFORM TO THE ANGLE OF THE WINDOW AND ALL PLEATS TO BE UPRIGHT. ALL BOTTOM HEMS TO BE LEVEL.

TIE-BACKS (WHERE SPECIFIED): One (1) pair of tie-backs for each pair of drapery, four (4) inches wide, length to be determined by finished width of drapery. Brass single zero grommet on each end.

DRAPERY TO BE PROPERLY DRESSED AND FAN-FOLDED, COMPLETELY DRESSED DOWN WHEN INSTALLED.

Marriott corporation INTERNATIONAL HEADQUARTERS MARRIOTT DRIVE WASHINGTON, D.C. 20058	SHEET TITLE UNLINED DRAPERY SPECIFICATIONS	DATE 8/12/88	DWG NO. 1 of 1

SATEEN LINED DRAPERY

ALL GOODS MUST BE INSPECTED FOR DEFECTS BEFORE CUTTING.

DRAPERIES TO BE CUSTOM TABLED FOR EXACT SIZE. ALL SELVAGE TO BE REMOVED. ALL PATTERNS MUST BE MATCHED.

SEAMS: FABRIC: Merrowed with overlock stitch using 100% polyester thread.
LINING: Merrowed with overlock stitch using 100% polyester thread.

HEADINGS: Buchram to be inserted between face fabric and lining, stitched across top. On overlaps and returns, double fold back of buckram is 12" on each. Lining to extend to top of finished drapery. ("Pillow Case Top")

BOTTOM HEMS: FABRIC: Double fold four (4) inch straight stitched, sewn closures at overlaps and returns, using 100% polyester thread. Lobbies and suites to be blindstitched using 100% polyester thread.
LINING: Two (2) inch straight stitched, single turn-up, finishing two (2) inches above face fabric, using 100% polyester thread. NOTE: All corners on bottom hem are to be mitered.

SIDE HEMS: Blind stitched one and one-half (1-1/2) inch with lining to edge of drapery, using 100% polyester thread.

WEIGHTS: FABRIC: One (1) inch covered lead weights tacked hem line on each seam and corner.
LINING: None required.

PLEATS: Triple fold French pleats machine sewn with 14 thread bar, "L" tack or "F" tack one-half (1/2) inch up from bottom of buckram, using #25 monofilament thread.

OVERLAPS: Three and one-half (3-1/2) inch with double fold back of buckram.

RETURNS: Three to six (3-6) inch depending on application with double fold back of buckram.

HOOKS: Pin on Kirsch #1012-C, Stainless Steel.

SLANT TOPS: IF SPECIFIED, ALL SLANT TOPS TO CONFORM TO THE ANGLE OF THE WINDOW AND ALL PLEATS TO BE UPRIGHT. ALL BOTTOM HEMS TO BE LEVEL.

DRAPERY TO BE FAN-FOLDED COMPLETELY DRESSED DOWN WHEN INSTALLED.

Marriott corporation INTERNATIONAL HEADQUARTERS MARRIOTT DRIVE WASHINGTON, D.C. 20058	SHEET TITLE SATEEN LINED DRAPERY SPECIFICATIONS	DATE 8/12/88	DWG NO. 1 of 1

1355 DRAPERY DESIGN CRITERIA—TYPICAL GUEST ROOMS

- ☐ Window treatments in typical rooms must include overdrapes, casements or sheets, and blackouts.

- ☐ Overdrapes may be full-traverse or side-hanging, dead hung or tied back, to complement the design format.

- ☐ Installation may be a two-track or three-track system. Three-track systems shall have individual tracks for sheers, blackouts and overdrapery. When fixed, side-hanging overdrapes are used, short tracks or rods approximately equal in length to the overdrapes are recommended.

- ☐ Two-track installations must consist of individual rods for sheers and full-traverse overdrapes with sewn-in blackout lining.

- ☐ Blackout material laminated to overdrapery is not permitted.

- ☐ Fabric valances are optional.

- ☐ 'Double-faced' portieres are optional.

HILTON	**1350 Interior Design Criteria—Guest Rooms**	
PLANNING AND DESIGN STANDARDS	November 1, 1989	1350–23

1356 DRAPERY FABRICATION SPECIFICATIONS

A. GENERAL INSTRUCTIONS

☐ Drapery contractor shall supply all labor, fittings, equipment, appliances and service necessary to furnish completed draperies required on all drawings and specification sheets.

☐ Drapery contractor shall provide proper storage for all owner-supplied fabrics, and shall maintain a current inventory records of same available to owner upon request. Evidence of adequate insurance shall be furnished.

☐ Drapery contractor shall be responsible for taking measurements at the job site and recording in writing any variations to the approximate sizes and styles specified herein. No variations, additions, or deletions shall be made by the subcontractor without a confirmed addendum to the contract issued by the Hotel.

☐ All draperies shall be made with the required widths of fabric specified, and never shall less than one-half of the width be used in any panel. Partial widths, when used, shall be sewn to the trailing end of the panel.

☐ Fitting and supplies, such as buckram, weights, thread and samples, shall be submitted to the Hotel, if requested, for approval before fabrication is started.

☐ Drapery samples and/or model room installations shall be provided by contractor on any type of drapery requested by the Hotel before fabrication of same is started.

☐ Contractor shall provide supervision and labor to perform acceptable fabrication and installation.

☐ Contractor shall make all necessary adjustments in the work as may be required to render the work in proper condition suitable for final acceptance. Acceptance will be given by a representative of the hotel for completed rooms or completed areas. Approval will not be given for incomplete rooms or incomplete areas. Approval will be in writing.

☐ All draperies shall be properly dressed and decorator-folded for delivery to job for installation.

B. INSPECTION AND FLAME RETARDING

☐ All fabric shall be shipped directly to the fabricator's workroom where they shall be inspected for flaws and/or defects before being put into work. Supplier is to be notified immediately of any significant flaws and/or defects. Significant flaws and/or defects are those which may cause a loss of fabric and/or necessitate replacement of goods. Final decision regarding fabric usage rests with the Hotel. Tags on all rolls listing yardage are to be available to owner for inspection. When the job is completed, the hotel is to be notified of any yardage left over. Fabric is to be safely stored or delivered to owner as requested.

☐ Draperies must have a 1/4" clearance at the ceiling mount.

☐ Bottom of draperies may vary from 1/4"–3/4" above the finished floor line and/or top of carpet, 1/2" clearance is recommended.

☐ See individual specifications for variances in general fabrication instructions.

☐ Thread tension must be adjusted according to fabric. Loose stitching will not be acceptable. Single needle stitch length shall be 6 to 9 per inch; adjusted to eliminate puckering.

☐ Material must meet the flameproofing standard as outlined in NFPA 701.

C. HANGING OF FINISHED DRAPERIES

☐ Buckram heading shall be forward creased between pleats prior to or during installation.

☐ All draperies shall be pinned and hung evenly with Kirsch #1012C stainless steel pins.

☐ All drapery returns shall be attached to wall with screw-hooks.

☐ All draperies shall be dressed down after hanging.

☐ All draperies, hardware and installation shall be provided in accordance with the enclosed specifications, and shall not have deviations other than orders written and issued by the hotel.

HILTON PLANNING AND DESIGN STANDARDS	1350 Interior Design Criteria— Guest Rooms	
	November 1, 1989	1350–25

D. OVERDRAPERY-UNLINED

☐ Draperies are to be custom-tabled for exact size. All selvages are to be removed. ALL PATTERNS MUST BE MATCHED.

☐ Fullness:

- 200% (two times the width of the opening when measured across the finished hem) plus overlaps and returns.

☐ Seams:

- Overlocked or merrowed (3/16") seams to be hidden behind pleats at headings.

☐ Headings:

- Single fold, tucked under, 4" with permanent finished buckram that ends at overlaps and returns. Sewn closures at overlaps and returns.

☐ Bottom Hems:

- Double fold 4" single needle stitching, sewn closures at overlaps and returns. Thread tension must be adjusted according to fabric. Loose stitching will not be acceptable.

☐ Weights:

- 1" covered lead weights tacked at hemline on each seam and each end.

☐ Pleats:

- Triple-fold French pleats machine-sewn 1" below buckram with 'L' tack 1/2" up from bottom of buckram.

☐ Overlaps:

- 3" with double fold of buckram.

☐ Returns:

- 30" or as needed to return to wall with double fold back or buckram.

☐ Hooks:

- Pin on Kirsch #1012C (stainless steel).

HILTON

PLANNING AND DESIGN STANDARDS

☐ Thread:

- All sewing to be with clear #25 monofilament high-heat thread.

- Draperies are to be properly dressed and decorator-folded, completely dressed down when installed (and tied back, if specified).

E. BLACKOUT DRAPERY

☐ Draperies are to be custom-tabled for exact size. All selvages are to be removed. Fabric is to be pleated on the cotton face, with suede or foam to the outside of the windows.

☐ Fullness:

- 200% (twice the width of the opening when measured across the finished hem) plus overlaps and returns.

☐ Seams:

- Self-bound or French seams to be hidden behind pleats at headings. Seams are not to leak light.

☐ Headings:

- Single fold, tucked under, 4" permanent-finished buckram-sewn closures at overlaps and returns.

☐ Bottom Hems:

- Reverse fold ('Z' fold) 4" self-faced double straight-stitched bottom hems with sewn closures at overlaps and return. Raw edges to be even with hem.

☐ Side Hems:

- Reverse fold ('Z' fold) 1–1/2" self-faced double straight-stitched. Raw edge to be tucked under.

☐ Weights:

- 1" covered lead weights tacked in hemline on each seam and each end.

HILTON

PLANNING AND DESIGN STANDARDS

1350 Interior Design Criteria— Guest Rooms
November 1, 1989	1350–27

☐ Pleats:

- Triple-fold French pleats machine-sewn with lock-stitch with 'L' tack 1/2" up from bottom of buckram.

☐ Overlaps:

- 3" with reverse fold-back of buckram. Installation in guest room is to place front of overlap on side with headboard wall so if there is any 'light leak' it is away from the bed.

☐ Returns:

- 3" or as needed to return to wall with double fold-back or buckram.

☐ Hooks:

- Pin on Kirsch #1012C.

☐ Thread:

- All sewing is to be with #25 monofilament high-heat thread or cotton mercerized fabric. Needle holes will not be accepted.

- Draperies are to be properly decorator-folded and completely dressed down when installed.

F. OVERDRAPERY LINED WITH BLACKOUT

☐ Drapery is to be custom-tabled for exact size. All selvages are to be removed. Blackout cotton back is to face the inside of the building, with vinyl or foam to the outside. OVERDRAPERY FABRIC MUST BE MATCHED.

☐ Fullness:

- 200% (two times the width of the opening when measured across the finished hem) plus overlaps and returns.

☐ Seams:

- 3/16" flat seams or overlocked, hidden behind pleats at headings.

HILTON

PLANNING AND DESIGN STANDARDS

1350 Interior Design Criteria— Guest Rooms

November 1, 1989 | 1350–28

☐ Headings:

- Double fold, permanent finish 4" buckram to be stitched at top of face goods, edge tucked under, blackout lining self-faced for continuous color appearance to outside of building, overdrape headings end at overlaps and returns, sewn closure (lined all the way up the back to top of heading).

☐ Bottom Hems:

- Overdraped to have double fold 4" single-needle stitching sewn closures at overlaps and returns.

- Blackout lining to have single fold 2–1/2" self-faced straight-stitch sewn closures at overlaps and returns. Hem to be 1–1/2" above finished drapery line. Blackout drapery lining hem to be independent of overdrapery hem.

☐ Side Hems:

- 1–1/2" face fabric on lining side.

☐ Weights:

- 1" covered lead weights tacked in hemline on each seam and each end.

☐ Pleats:

- Overdrape to have triple-fold French pleats machine-sewn 1" below buckram with 'L' tack 1/2" up from bottom of buckram.

☐ Overlaps:

- 3" with double fold back of buckram.

☐ Returns:

- 3" or as needed to return to wall with double fold back of buckram.

☐ Hooks:

- Pin on Kirsch #1012C (Stainless steel).

- Draperies are to be properly dressed and decorator-folded and completely dressed down when installed (and tied back, if specified).

HILTON

PLANNING AND DESIGN STANDARDS

G. DRAPERY HARDWARE

☐ Hardware to be used is listed below. These numbers pertain to Kirsch hardware or equal (submit sample and specification).

☐ USING #9095 CUSTOM DOUBLE-DUTY SYSTEM FOR ALL TRAVERSE DRAPERY:

- #9095: Track double-duty rodding formed from 0.030" steel, precoated, baked enamel, with white finish; amount is footage per track, cut to measure.

- #9287: Ball bearing pulley set; 1 per set.

- #9495: Plain side; 3 each foot.

- #9487: Two-way reversible arm master (for center-opening drapes); 1 pair.

- #9492: One way reversible master (for one-way draw, left or right); 1 each.

- #9923: Cord tension pulley; 1 each.

- #9906: Size #4 traverse cord, nylon braided traverse cord; number of widths doubled and height doubled.

- #3315: Double brackets, for wall mount installation; 1 each.

- #9595: Double support, for wall mount installation; 1 every 3 feet (i.e., 4 for 12 feet).

- #9597: Ceiling stirrups, used for ceiling installation (concrete, sheet rock, plaster, etc.); 1 every 3 feet.

- #1787: #8 1–1/2" plated-type screw on all installations except metal.

- #1012C: Stainless steel drapery hook to insure that flameretarding of fabric does not cause rusting; pins are used in all draperies; 1 each pleat and end.

☐ USING #9095 CUSTOM DOUBLE-DUTY SYSTEM FOR STATIONARY DRAPERY (TIEBACK AND VALANCE):

- #9095: Track-same as previously listed; amount is footage per track, cut to measure.

- #9495: Plain slide; 3 each foot.

HILTON

PLANNING AND DESIGN STANDARDS

- #9494: Lock slide; 2 each.

- #9597: Ceiling stirrup-same as previously listed; 2 each.

- #1012C: Stainless steel drapery hook to insure that flameretarding of fabric does not cause rusting; pins are used in all draperies; 1 each pleat and end.

- #7651R: Concealed holder for tiebacks with large returns; 1 per drape.

☐ USING #94008 ARCHITRAC CUSTOM CORDLESS HAND-DRAW TRACK FOR ALL HAND-PULL BLACKOUT, SHEER, OR LINED OVERDRAPE:

- #94008: Track hand-draw; amount is footage per track. Cut to measure. Note: In humid or ocean climates, #94003 must be used.

- #9670: Architrac ball bearing carrier; 1 per set.

- #9683: End stops; 1 pair each.

- #94133 RH: Master carrier for architrac hand-draw traverse; 1 each.

- #94134 LH: Master carrier for architrac hand-draw traverse; 1 each.

- #3558–25: Ceiling clip for 94008 rod, 1 every 3 feet.

- #94140: Ceiling clip for 94003; 1 every 3 feet.

- #91233: Color #25, 3 foot fiberglass baton, 3/8" diameter.

- #94110: Splice, if needed (for 94003 only).

- #94145: Overlap stiffener with eyelet.

- #8460–812: Stanley, for tieback screw-hook.

- "O"GROMMET: Brass grommet and washer for tieback.

H. UPHOLSTERED CORNICE

☐ Fabricate using minimum 1/2" plywood with minimum 1" x 3" frame top and returns.

☐ All staples and/or tacks are to be corrosion-resistant type that will inhibit rust caused by flame retardant fabrics and/or humidity. All staples and/or tacks are to be covered from view.

☐ Welting or trim, if required, is to be attached in a manner such as to ensure that it maintains a straight line.

☐ All padding will be flame retardant; 1/2" flame retardant foam is acceptable unless otherwise specified.

☐ Cornice will be self-lined unless otherwise specified. All raw edges of wood shall be covered.

☐ Mounting method to be determined by drapery contractor using most secure and appropriate method.

I. SHEER OR CASEMENT DRAPERY

☐ Draperies must be custom-tabled for exact size. All selvages to be removed. ALL PATTERNS MUST BE MATCHED.

☐ Fullness: 250% (2–1/2 times the width of the opening when measured across the finished hem) plus overlaps and returns.

☐ Seams: Overlocked or merrowed (3/16") seams to be hidden behind pleat at headings.

☐ Headings: Double fold 4" with permanent-finished buckram ends at overlaps and returns, sewn closures.

☐ Bottom Hems: Double fold 4" straight-stitched. Sewn closures at overlaps and returns. Exception: On fabrics with a weighted selvage that may be railroaded, the weighted edge as woven on the fabric will be considered a finish hem.

☐ Side Hems: Double fold 1–1/2" straight-stitched.

☐ Weights: 1" covered lead weights tacked in hem line on each seam and each end or solid bead hem. Hem shall be even and will not bow due to weights.

☐ Pleats: Triple fold French pleats machine-sewn 1" below buckram "L" tack 1/2" up from bottom of buckram.

☐ Overlaps: 3" with double fold back of buckram.

☐ Returns: 3" or as needed to return to wall with double fold back of buckram.

☐ Hooks: Pin on Kirsch #1012C stainless steel pins.

HILTON
PLANNING AND DESIGN STANDARDS

☐ Draperies to be properly dressed and decorator-folded, completely dressed down when installed.

☐ NOTE: If Gardisette casement draperies are to be fabricated by Gardisette, it will be the drapery contractor's responsibility to provide finished dimensions to Gardisette and install the same draperies, providing hardware as required. Gardisette pinning system is to be used.

1357 BEDSPREAD AND/OR DRAPERY FABRIC SPECIFICATIONS

A. BEDSPREAD AND/OR OVERDRAPERY FABRIC

☐ Width: Minimum 45" width (54" preferred)

☐ Weight: Minimum 190 (1.9 yd./lb.)

☐ Print: Vat-dyed or fiber reactive colors only (preshrunk). All colors must have vat fastness. Pigment colors not allowed.

☐ Weave: Warp-sateen, sheeting or duck.

☐ Maximum shrinkage: Allowed 2–3%.

☐ Flameretardant: Overdrapery fabric must meet all local codes, as well as N.F.P.A. 701 small-scale test for drapery application.

☐ Content: 100% cotton preferred.

☐ 100% polyester fabric for drapery is not permitted without prior approval from Hilton.

B. DRAPERY BLACKOUT FABRIC

☐ Either of the following is acceptable:

- TWO-PASS SOFT BLACKOUT LINING—RECOMMENDED MINIMUM FOR GUEST ROOMS
  — Width: 48" or 54"
  — Weight: 1.45 yds./lb. (48"w)
  — Color: Exterior white or ecru-interior off-white or light gray.
  — Fiber Content and Process: 50% cotton/50% polyester with two "foam" passes to create blackout.
  — Thread count: 78 x 54 per square inch or equal.

HILTON
PLANNING AND DESIGN STANDARDS

Corporate Specification Example

713.0 Lamps: All fixtures (shades, etc.) must be rated to accommodate the required bulb wattages.

    a. A bed lamp with individual directive light and control is required. If twin light fixtures between beds are used, they must have at least 75 watt bulbs in each socket; a single bulb fixture between beds must be no less then 100 watt incandescent.

    b. Lounge area lamp is to be compatible with the design of the lamps, and must have a minimum of one 100 watt soft white incandescent bulb.

    c. Desk-dresser lamp must have at least one 100 watt bulb and be compatible with the other lamps.

    d. A wall switch at the room entrance must be provided to operate at least one lamp. All table lamps must have a weighted base with switch. Lamp fixtures are to be of good quality and well coordinated with the other furnishings in the room. Control switches, mounted bedside are recommended for handicapped rooms.

713.1 Lamp Shades: All lamp shades must be translucent white or linen. The light reflecting or restricting characteristics of the lamp shade must be evaluated with the ultimate judgment of acceptability being made on the adequacy of illumination for reading.

714.0 Mirrors: A framed, wall-mounted mirror, complementing the room design must be provided in the sleeping area of the room, in addition to that required in the bath/vanity area. The minimum glass surface shall be 24" × 36". Mirror is to be located over the dresser.

715.0 Wall Decor: Adequate wall decor (framed pictures or similar) must be provided to complement room decor. Two pictures are required in rooms with more than one bed. Minimum required size is 20" × 24". At least one picture of minimum size 30" × 30" is required in one-bedded rooms. Recommended are anti-theft clips for mounting wall decor in lieu of visible screw mounting. In rooms where sofa beds are used, two framed pictures of minimum size 20" × 24" are required.

716.0 Carpeting: Floors must receive quality wall to wall carpeting over a separate quality pad. All carpeting must have a minimum face weight of 28 ounces. Carpeting and pad must meet industry standards for flame spread rating.

717.0 Draperies: Drapes may be center or side draw, on one or multiple tracks. Drapes must be of sufficient size and fullness that they fully cover window—vertically and horizontally—and do not gap when closed. Drapes must have black-out capability. Length of drape must be sufficient to help achieve black-out effect. Heavy duty, commercial grade hardware is required. While heavy duty draw cords are permitted, hand wands are recommended for most applications.

718.0 Mattress Pads: All beds are to be furnished with a pad for the mattress. The pad must be of a correct size and fitted or corner-strapped to prevent slippage. Pads are to be of one piece construction (no seams) and machine washable and dryable. Filler shall be of high quality; the top surface absorbent; the bottom surface moisture resistant. Either smooth or quilted surface is acceptable, depending upon materials. Anti-static material is preferred. Foam pads are not acceptable.

719.0 Pillows: All beds are to be furnished with pillows, including rollaways and sofa-sleepers. Double and queen-size beds must have two pillows. King-size beds must have two king-size pillows (or three standard pillows). Additional pillows are to be provided in the room or in storage, available upon request by the guest. Pillow quality must be equal to or exceed the following standards:

    a. Feather filled: A minimum blend of 80% feather and 20% goose or duck down. Blue and white stripe cotton ticking. 107 × 76 thread count per square inch, with corded tailored edging. Fire retardant.

    b. Polyester fiber: 100% 20 ounce virgin polyester, batted to specifications with corded tailored edging. Machine washable and dryable. Fire retardant.

    c. Polyurethane fill: Polyurethane flaked fiber fill. Blue and white stripe cotton linen finish cover, with corded tailored edging. Machine washable and dryable. Fire retardant. Solid foam pillows are not acceptable.

Taken from the Choice Hotels International, Inc. Rules and Regulations. Q: 1–88 Page 19, Specifications 713.0–719.0, Reprinted with permission.

Feasibility Study

(Note: This is a summary of a rather lengthy document. It does as-
sess for the owner, operator, architectural and design teams,
the pertinent information.)

II. SUMMARY OF CONCLUSIONS

Our study and analysis of the available information indicate
that there is a market for a 165-room all-suite hotel located in
southwest Fort Myers, Florida. Assuming contemporary design, com-
petent management, effective promotion and major chain affiliation,
the proposed Hotel could anticipate successful market penetration,
acceptable levels of occupancy and average room rate. The following
comments specifically highlight the findings that support these con-
clusions:

- Lee County has exhibited significant economic growth
  in recent years. The geographic, economic and
  demographic factors which were reviewed, coupled
  with projections by various public and private sec-
  tor planners, point to a continuation of strong
  growth throughout the 1985 to 1990 period.

- The southwest Fort Myers area is clearly in the
  development path. The opening of Summerlin Road has
  encouraged residential, retail, and commercial development in the newly accessible south western region.

- The attributes of the subject site at the intersec-
  tion of Summerlin and Bunch Beach Roads, including
  location, accessibility, visibility, ingress/egress
  and site characteristics, are all supportive of successful hotel development. However, strategically
  placed directional signs will be necessary to ensure adequate exposure to traveling motorists.

- The proposed Hotel, as the first chain-affiliated
  property in the southwestern Fort Myers area, will
  not compete directly with an existing market supply. Instead, it will compete indirectly with other
  chain-affiliated or quality hotels located in the
  South Fort Myers, Cape Coral, and Fort Myers Beach
  market sectors.

- Nine existing lodging properties containing 1,162
  guest rooms should be indirectly competitive with

the proposed Hotel. These properties offer facilities and services of varying size, scope, and quality.

· Annual occupancies at competitive properties in 1984 are estimated to range from 30 percent to 79 percent, with a composite average of 55 percent. The 1984 demand base for the competitive properties is estimated to be approximately 223,600 room nights.

· Occupancies vary significantly by season, with area hotels operating near capacity levels during the 89-day peak winter season.

· At certain times during the winter season, as well as on holiday weekends and during special area events, the demand for hotel rooms exceeds the available supply of accommodations. This demand is turned away to nonchain-affiliated properties, other lodging alternatives and, to a lesser extent, hotels in other sectors.

· Average room rates for the competitive supply are estimated to range from $28 to $65 in 1984, with a composite average of $41. Market segmentation is as follows:

Segment	Percent of lodging demand
Tourist	48%
Group	3
Commercial	49
	100%

· While the projected 1984 market area occupancy represents a decrease from that experienced in 1983 due to the addition of three hotels to the supply, the number of occupied room nights in the market area increased over 30 percent during that period.

· We project future growth rates of this demand base at the following rates:

Year	Composite growth rate
1985	13%
1986	14
1987	9
1988	7
1989	3
1990	2

· While there are several proposed hotels in the Fort Myers area, we are aware of no additions to the supply that are considered competitive to the proposed Hotel.

· Proposed facilities for the subject property include the following:

  .. 165 guest suites.

  .. Outdoor swimming pool.

  .. Vending machines.

  .. Guest laundry facilities.

  .. A lounge.

· We assume the subject Hotel's first full operating year to be 1986. Our projections of occupancy and average room rates are for the proposed Hotel's first five full years of operation, 1986 to 1990.

Year	Occupancy percentage*	Average room rate 1985 dollars	Average room rate Inflated	Total room sales* (inflated)
1986	62%	$42	$45	$1,686,000
1987	66	45	52	2,035,000
1988	70	47	57	2,408,000
1989	71	47	61	2,608,000
1990	71	47	66	2,832,000

*Rounded.

Source: Laventhol & Horwath.

· Based on the utilization levels expressed above, we have projected total sales and cash flows from operations available for incentive management fee, debt service and income taxes to be as follows:

Year	Total sales (inflated)	Cash flow from operations available for incentive management fee, debt service and income taxes (inflated)
1986	$1,897,000	$ 719,000
1987	2,276,000	931,000
1988	2,680,000	1,153,000
1989	2,904,000	1,263,000
1990	3,152,000	1,388,000

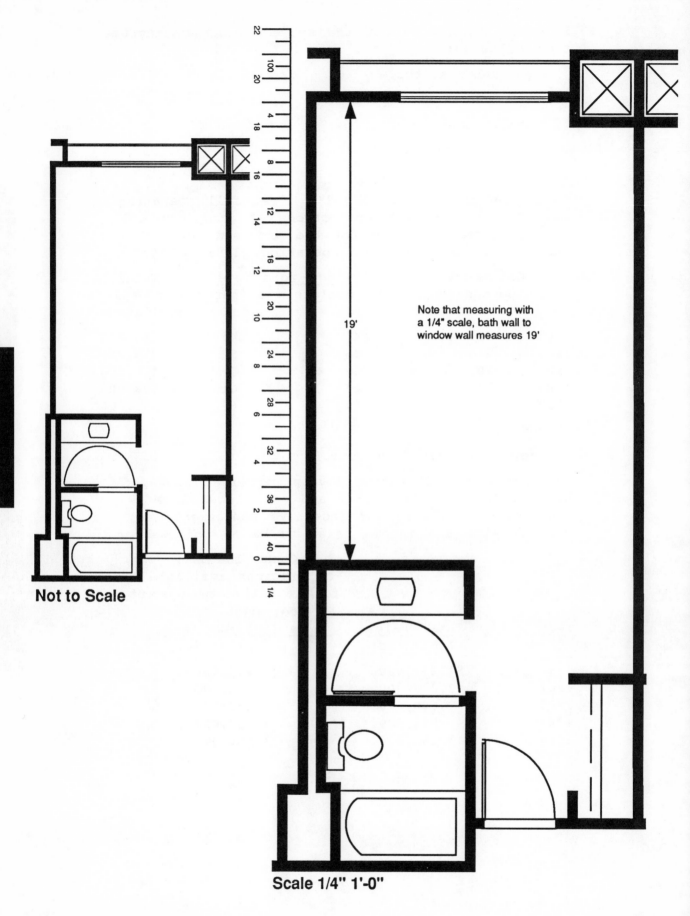

Note that measuring with a 1/4" scale, bath wall to window wall measures 19'

19'

Not to Scale

Scale 1/4" 1'-0"

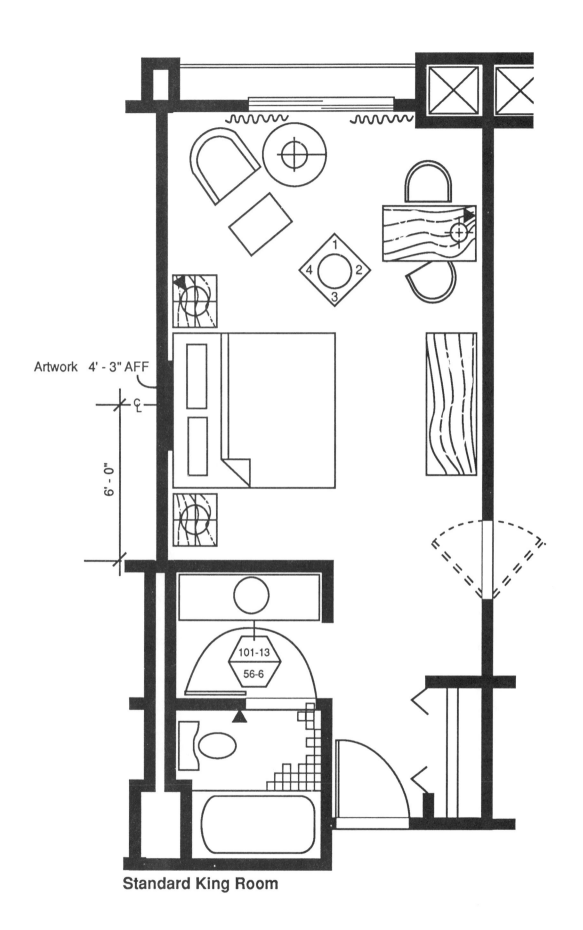

Artwork 4' - 3" AFF

¢

6' - 0"

101-13
56-6

Standard King Room

FF&E Standard Size Chart

Beds Sizes

California King	72"W × 84"L (also known as Western King)
Regular King	78"W × 80"L (also known as Dual King)
Double	54"W × 75"L (also known as Full)
Queen	60"W × 80"L
Twin	39"W × 75"L
Youth Bed	33"W × 66"L
Roll-Away Bed	38"W × 80"L

Bedspread Drop: Top of bed to floor. Most beds have a standard drop from the edge of the mattress to the floor of 20" to 21". Field measuring is important as mattress and bed heights do vary.

Pillow Sizes

Standard	26"L × 20"W
Queen	30"L × 20"W
King	36"L × 20"W

Seating

Seat height for Desk Chair	19" to 19-1/2"
Seat height for Dining Chair	18" to 19-1/2"
Seat height for Comfortable Chair	17" to 19"
Seat height for Bar Stools	30"
Sofa Length	82" to 89"
Love Seat Length	60" to 66"

Furnishings

These sizes will vary with different styles, but these are average sizes to help with elevation drawings.

Desk Height	29" to 29-1/2"
Dining Table Height	29"
Cocktail Table Height	15-1/2" to 18"
Sofa Table Height	27" to 29"
End Table Height	22" to 26"
Nightstand Height	23" to 27"
Dresser Height	31" to 34"
Low Credenza Height	29" to 31"
Armoir Height	82" to 84"

Sliding Glass Door (One-Way Draw)	6'
End Panels	30"
O.D. Drapery Length	84"
Sheer Length	83-1/2" (always 1/2" shorter than overdrapes)
Valance Length	12" (based on 84" length overdrapes)

Estimation of Wallcovering and Carpet

Estimating Wallcovering:

The formula for estimating the quantity of wallcovering material needed for a guestroom is based on the number of square feet on the roll. Many wallcoverings are packaged in single rolls of 36 square feet (3.4 sq. m) or double roll of 72 square feet (6.7 sq. m). Usually the bookcover or sample will give you this information.

Measurements of the interior space of the room are made in feet, noting the number of windows, doors and other major architectural features, i.e. fireplace. For example, in estimating the wallcovering needed for a 14' x 14' room with 9' ceilings, two windows and a door, you would proceed as follows:

1. Measure the length of each wall, add and total.

   14' + 14' + 14' + 14' = 56'

2. Multiple the distance around the room by the ceiling height to determine the total number of square feet.

   56' × 9' = 504 Square Feet

3. Allow a 20 percent margin for waste.

   504 Square Feet + 20% = 604.8 Square Feet

4. Calculate the actual areas for doors, windows and other architectural features. Allow 15 feet as an average size per door and for every two windows.

   2 × 15 Square Feet = 30 Square Feet for window allowance, plus 15 for the door = 45 sq. ft. total

5. Subtract the area for doors, windows and other architectural features.

   604 Square Feet minus 45 Square Feet = 559 Square Feet

The last figure represents the total number of square feet of wallcovering that is required to complete the space, and from it the number of rolls can be determined.

If the selected wallcovering is packaged in standard rolls of 36 Square Feet:

559 Divided by 36 Square Feet per Roll = 15.53 or 16 single rolls.

The amount needed would be 16 single rolls or 8 double rolls. In the event that the wallcovering is packaged in rolls containing 30 square feet, the project would require more wallcovering, i.e. 574.8 divided by 30 square feet = 19.16 or 20 single rolls. In this case, the project would require 20 single rolls or 10 double rolls.

Designers should remember that uneven figures should always be increased to the next highest number. If the wallcovering is only packaged in double rolls, the figures may have to be increased to the next highest even number: 6.4 rolls would be increased to 8 double rolls.

Vinyl Wallcovering

Because commercial vinyls are packaged in 30 yard bolts, ranging from 52 to 54 inches in width, the estimation may be made in square feet, linear feet or yards. The most common method used to calculate yardage in fabric wallcoverings is explained below. If the designer wishes to make the calculation in square feet, the square footage of a bolt can be made in the following manner:

13.5 square feet per yard × 30 yards = 405 square feet per bolt

Using the same footage requirements from the previous example:

574.8 Divided by 405 Square Feet per Bolt = 1.41 Bolts or 2 Bolts

Estimating Carpet Quantities

When estimating carpet quantities for guestrooms, you will primarily be dealing with solid carpets or very small print, so your allowances will be minimal. Take footage of the full length × the footage of the width and divide by 9. This will give you the equivalent square yards, which is the way guestroom carpet is sold.

Bath areas with tiled surfaces should be subtracted from this figure to give you a more accurate figure. A guestroom that is 12' × 36' equals 432 square feet; divide this by 9 and you will see that you need 48 square yards of carpet for the guestroom.

Note: When working on renovation or new construction, remember that you can use these formulas to develop approximate figures. *All Items* should be *field measured* prior to ordering vinyl, carpet, bedspreads, tile, etc., because sizes will change from manufacturer to manufacturer and oftentimes blueprints and plans can vary slightly from the actual room—enough so as not to give accurate room measurements. It would be wise to add to your specification sheets that give quantities "TO BE FIELD MEASURED BY INSTALLER".

The exercises presented are for your own use, to aid in producing *accurate* budget figures for your guestroom design. *Actual quantities* should only be given by the General Contractor.

5

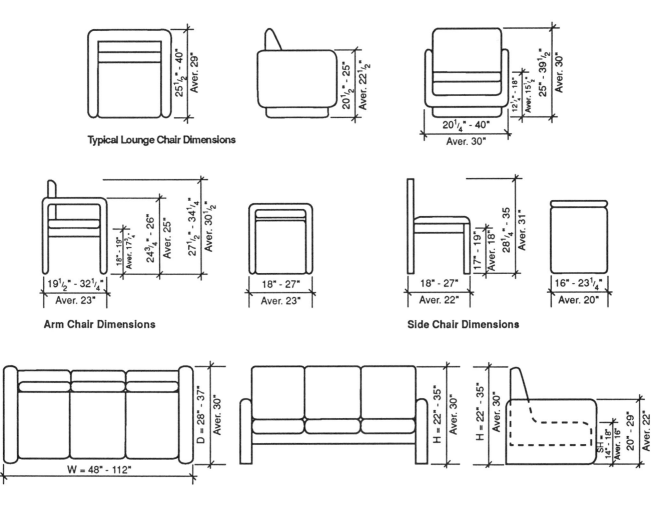

Typical Lounge Chair Dimensions

Arm Chair Dimensions

Side Chair Dimensions

Typical Sofa Dimensions

Typical End or Side Table Dimensions (in.)

Description	Depth		Width		Height	
	Min.	Max.	Min.	Max.	Min.	Max.
Rectangular	19	28	21	48	17	28
Square	15	32	15	32	17	28
Round	16	30	16	30	18	22½

Typical Low Table Dimensions (in.)

Description	Depth		Width		Height	
	Min.	Max.	Min.	Max.	Min.	Max.
Rectangular	15½	24	21	56	12	18
Square	36	42	32	42	15	17
Round	30	42	20	42	15	16½

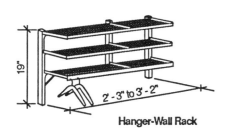

Hanger-Wall Rack

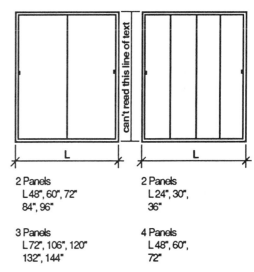

2 Panels
L 48", 60", 72"
84", 96"

2 Panels
L 24", 30",
36"

3 Panels
L 72", 106", 120"
132", 144"

4 Panels
L 48", 60",
72"

Sliding - Bifold Mirrored Closet Doors

5

SQUARE YARD TABLE
Up to 100 Lineal Ft. 12' and 15' Widths
Feet and Inches Reduced to Square Yards

Inches	12' 16/4	15' 20/4	Feet	12' 16/4	15' 20/4
Lineal Inches	*sq. yds.*	*sq. yds.*	*Lineal Feet*	*sq. yds.*	*sq. yds.*
1......	.11	.14	44.....	58.67	73.33
2......	.22	.28	45.....	60.00	75.00
3......	.33	.42	46.....	61.33	76.67
4......	.44	.56	47.....	62.67	78.33
5......	.55	.70	48.....	64.00	80.00
6......	.66	.84	49.....	65.33	81.67
7......	.78	.97	50.....	66.67	83.33
8......	.89	1.11	51.....	68.00	85.00
9......	1.00	1.25	52.....	69.33	86.67
10......	1.11	1.39	53.....	70.67	88.33
11......	1.22	1.53	54.....	72.00	90.00
Feet	**12'** 16/4	**15'** 20/4	55.....	73.33	91.67
			56.....	74.67	93.33
Lineal Inches	*sq. yds.*	*sq. yds.*	57.....	76.00	95.00
1......	1.33	1.67	58.....	77.33	96.67
2......	2.67	3.33	59.....	78.67	98.33
3......	4.00	5.00	60.....	80.00	100.00
4......	5.33	6.67	61.....	81.33	101.67
5......	6.67	8.33	62.....	82.67	103.33
6......	8.00	10.00	63.....	84.00	105.00
7......	9.33	11.67	64.....	85.33	106.67
8......	10.67	13.33	65.....	86.67	108.33
9......	12.00	15.00	66.....	88.00	110.00
10......	13.33	16.67	67.....	89.33	111.67
11......	14.67	18.33	68.....	90.67	113.33
12......	16.00	20.00	69.....	92.00	115.00
13......	17.33	21.67	70.....	93.33	116.67
14......	18.67	23.33	71.....	94.67	118.33
15......	20.00	25.00	72.....	96.00	120.00
16......	21.33	26.67	73.....	97.33	121.67
17......	22.67	28.33	74.....	98.67	123.33
18......	24.00	30.00	75.....	100.00	125.00
19......	25.33	31.67	76.....	101.33	126.67
20......	26.67	33.33	77.....	102.67	128.33
21......	28.00	35.00	78.....	104.00	130.00
22......	29.33	36.67	79.....	105.33	131.67
23......	30.67	38.33	80.....	106.67	133.33
24......	32.00	40.00	81.....	108.00	135.00
25......	33.33	41.67	82.....	109.33	136.67
26......	34.67	43.33	83.....	110.67	138.33
27......	36.00	45.00	84.....	112.00	140.00
28......	37.33	46.67	85.....	113.33	141.67
29......	38.67	48.33	86.....	114.67	143.33
30......	40.00	50.00	87.....	116.00	145.00
31......	41.18	51.67	88.....	117.33	146.67
32......	42.67	53.33	89.....	118.67	148.33
33......	44.00	55.00	90.....	120.00	150.00
34......	45.33	56.67	91.....	121.33	151.67
35......	46.67	58.33	92.....	122.67	153.33
36......	48.00	60.00	93.....	124.00	155.00
37......	49.33	61.67	94.....	125.33	156.67
38......	50.67	63.33	95.....	126.67	158.33
39......	52.00	65.00	96.....	128.00	160.00
40......	53.33	66.67	97.....	129.33	161.67
41......	54.67	68.33	98.....	130.67	163.33
42......	56.00	70.00	99.....	132.00	165.00
43.....	57.33	71.67	100.....	133.33	166.67

5

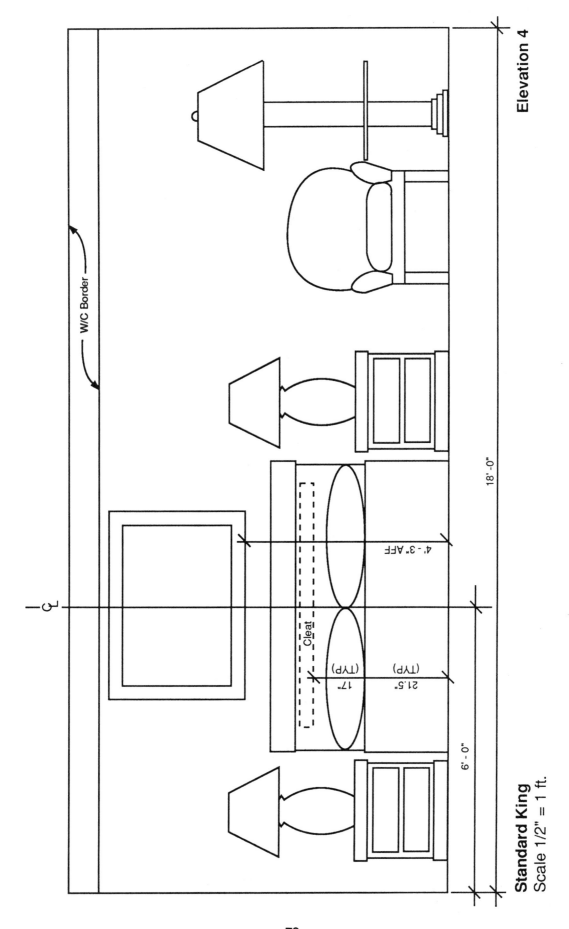

Standard King
Scale 1/2" = 1 ft.

Elevation 4

W/C Border

Cleat

17" (TYP)

21.5" (TYP)

4'-3" AFF

18'-0"

6'-0"

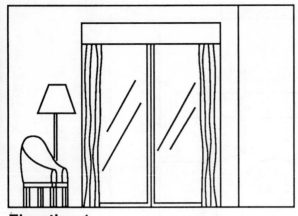

Elevation 1

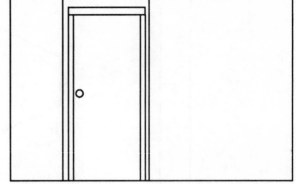

Elevation 3

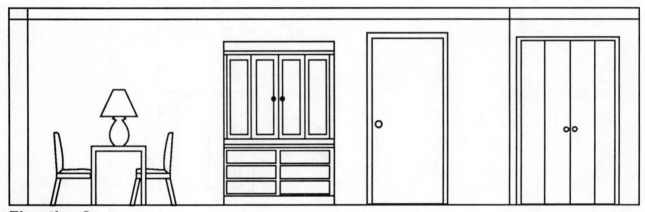

Elevation 2
No Scale

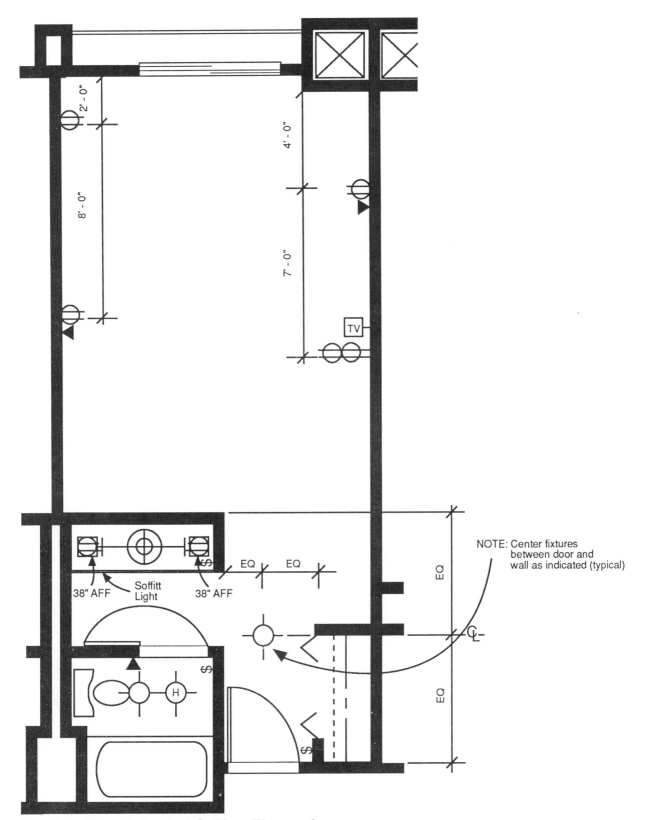

2' - 0"

8' - 0"

4' - 0"

7' - 0"

TV

NOTE: Center fixtures
between door and
wall as indicated (typical)

EQ

EQ

C L

38" AFF   Soffitt   38" AFF
Light

EQ   EQ

Combination Reflected Ceiling Plan and Electrical Plan Standard King Guestroom

Scale 1/4" = 1 ft.

Symbols

Interior
Elevation
Reference --- Wall Number

Room
Reference --- Room Number

Revision
Reference --- Revision Number

Detail
Reference --- Int. Design Page Number
--- Area - Detail Number

Abbreviations

CPT.	Carpet
EQUIP.	Equipment
EQ.	Equal
ADJ.	Adjustable
G.C.	General Contractor
N.I.C.	Not In Contract
O.F.C.I.	Owner Furnish/Contractor Install
AFF	Above Finish Floor
DWGS.	Drawings
W/	With
TYP.	Typical
WD.	Wood
PL.	Plastic Laminate
S/S	Stainless Steel
V.C.T.	Vinyl Composition Tile
W/C	Wall Covering
V.W.C.	Vinyl Wallcovering
STD.	Standard
RPT.	Repeat
T.B.D.	To Be Determined
₵L	Center Line

Architectural Graphic Standard Symbols

Lighting Outlets

Ceiling	Wall	
○	─○	Surface Incandescent
⊛	─⊛	Recess Incandescent
Ⓔ	─Ⓔ	Electrical Outlet
Ⓕ	─Ⓕ	Fan Outlet
Ⓙ	─Ⓙ	Junction Box
Ⓛps	─Ⓛps	Lamp Holder w/Pull Switch
Ⓧ	─Ⓧ	Exit Light Outlet

　[○]　Surface or Pendant Individual Flourescent Fixture

　[○R]　Recessed Individual Flourescent Fixture

　[○　　]　Surface or Pendant Continuous Row Flourescent Fixture

　[○R　　]　Recessed Continuous Row Flourescent Fixture

Receptacle Outlets

⊖	Single Receptacle Outlet
⧢	Duplex Receptacle Outlet
⧢	Triple Receptacle Outlet
⊕	Quadruplex Receptacle Outlet
©	Clock Hanger Receptacle
℗	Fan Hanger Receptacle
[◯]	Floor Single Receptacle Outlet
[◯]	Floor Duplex Receptacle Outlet
[△]	Floor Special Purpose Outlet

Switch Outlets

S	Single Pole Switch
S2	Double Pole Switch
S3	Triple Pole Switch
SCB	Circuit Breaker
ST	Timed Switch
Ⓢ	Ceiling Pull Switch
⊖S	Switch & Single Receptacle
⊖S	Switch & Double Receptacle

8

Signaling System Outlets

◄   Outside Telephone

▢◄   Telephone Switchboard

Ⓜ   Maids Signal Plug

Ⓡ   Radio Outlets

CH   Chime

TV   Television Outlet

Ⓣ   Thermostat

Miscellaneous & Graphic Symbols for Architectural Drawings

▥   Floor Register

Door Swing Symbols

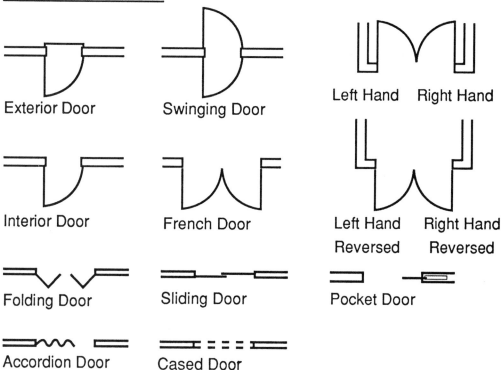

Exterior Door   Swinging Door   Left Hand   Right Hand

Interior Door   French Door   Left Hand   Right Hand
                                          Reversed   Reversed

Folding Door   Sliding Door   Pocket Door

Accordion Door   Cased Door

8

Stair Direction Symbol

 North Point
to be Placed on Each
Floor Plan, Generally
in Lower Right Hand
Corner of Drawing

 Indication Arrows
Drawn with Straight
Lines (Not Curved);
Must Touch Object

 Match Line
Shaded Portions - The Side
Considered

 Level Line
Control Point or Datum

 Revision

 Window Type

 Column Reference Grids

 Building Section
Reference Drawing Number

 Wall Section or Elevation
Reference Drawing Number

 Detail
Reference Drawing Number

1302 Room/Space Number

354 Equipment Number

 Project North
(Magnetic North Arrow Used on Plot Site
Plan Only)

 Door Number
(If More Than One Door Per Room Subscript
Letters Are Used)

Linework

Dash and Dot ⌐
Center Lines, Projections, Ext. Elevation Lines

Dash and Double Dot Line ⌐
Property Lines, Boundary Lines

Dotted Line ⌐
Hidden, Future or Existing Const. to be Removed

Break Line ⌐
To Break Off Parts of Drawing

Section Lines and Section References

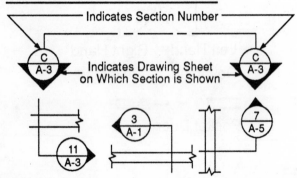

Detail References

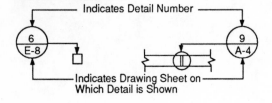

Horizontal Dimension Lines

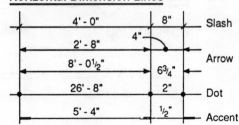

Vertical Dimension Lines

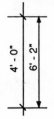

8

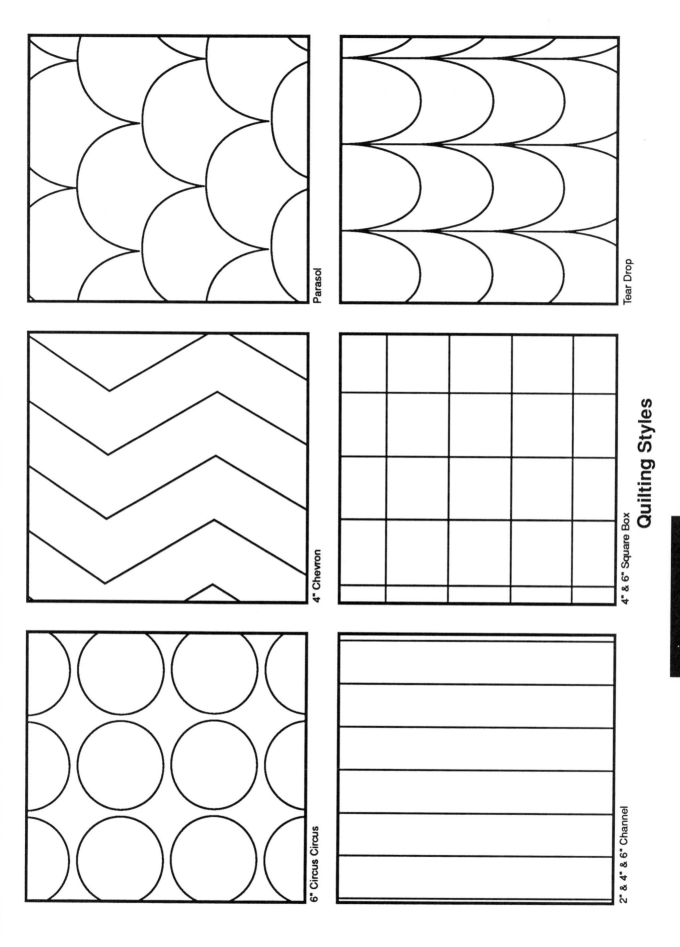

Parasol

Tear Drop

4" Chevron

4" & 6" Square Box

6" Circus Circus

2" & 4" & 6" Channel

Quilting Styles

ADDENDUM 9

Double Onion

Single Onion

Grecian

Vermicelli

1 x 3 Stripe

6" Diamond

Quilting Styles

9

Bedcover
Styles

Style A
Comforter, outline or hand guided pattern quilting, with square corners and 6" puff border on four sides.

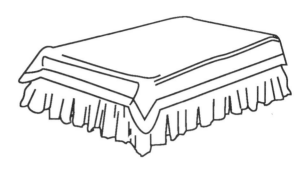

Style B
Throw style with rounded corners.

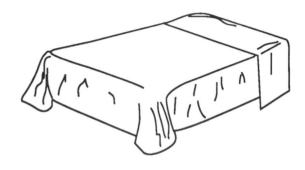

Style C
Fitted tailored bedspread, open corners with inserts. Welting on the top and 2" hem on the bottom.

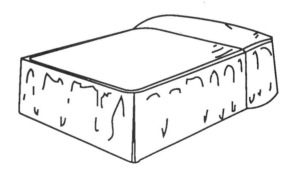

Style D
Fitted tailored bedspread style, open corners with inserts. No welting on the top and 2" hem on the bottom.

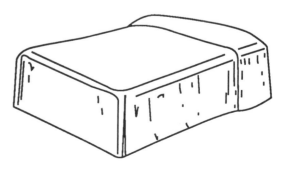

9

Coverlets

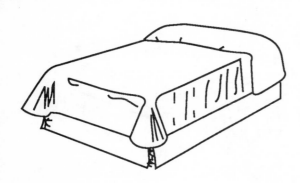

Style A
A throw coverlet with hem, straight drop and bell corners.

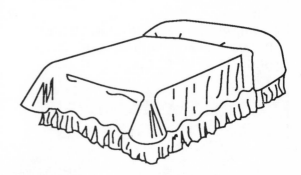

Style D
Scalloped throw coverlet, separately lined with sateen.

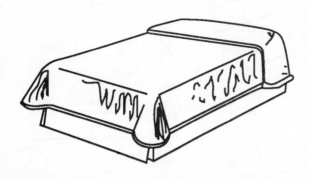

Style B
A throw coverlet with straight sides, jumbo 3/4" welting on the bottom, and bell corners.

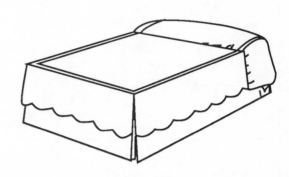

Style E
Tailored coverlet, welted top, open corners with inserts, separately lined with sateen.

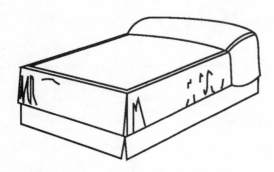

Style C
Tailored coverlet, welting top and open corners with inserts, straight sides.

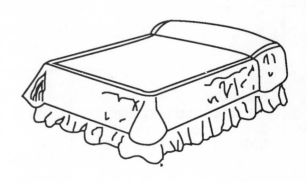

Style F
Combination fitted coverlet, welted top, bell corners and 2" hem on the bottom.

Dust Ruffles

Style 3

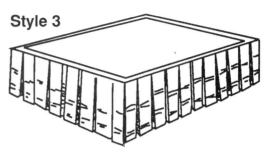

4" Box Pleated Duster With Facing on Top

Style 1

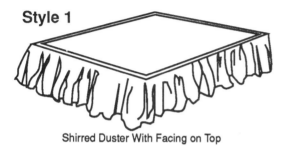

Shirred Duster With Facing on Top

Style 4

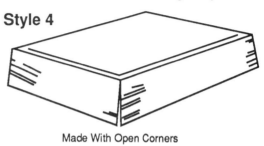

Made With Open Corners

Style 2

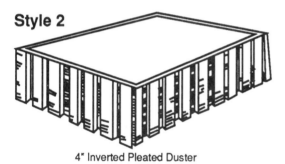

4" Inverted Pleated Duster

Style 5

Made With Closed Kick Plate

9

SPECTRUM
S E R V I C E S

SPECIFICATIONS

PROJECT: TENAYA MARRIOTT	**PAGE** 1 **OF** 1	S7-Da/S7-D
LOCATION: STANDARD GUESTROOMS	5/30/89	S7-DA/S7-D
	DATE	**ITEM#**

ITEM: Bedspread, Double

QUANTITY: 318

SUPPLIER: To Be Determined

MODEL: Throw Style

FINISH: 8 oz. poly fill, cotton back, 4" channel quilt

SIZE: To Fit Bed 54 x 80, 20-21" Drop and 20" Pillow Tuck

SUPPLIER: Schumacher

PATTERN: Spanish Colonial Tapestry

COLOR: Plum

CONTENT: 58% Linen/42% Cotton*

WIDTH: 54"

REPEAT: 25 1/4" Vertical

UNIT YARDAGE: 7 3/4 Yards Approx.

TOTAL YARDAGE: 2,544 Yards

See S7-D and S7-Da for fabrication specifications.

* Linen-Look/cotton fabric will be considered.

A D D E N D U M 10

RESTAURANT AND HOTEL INTERIORS
710 TERMINAL TOWER, CLEVELAND, OHIO 44113 (216)241-8450

SPECTRUM
S E R V I C E S

SPECIFICATIONS

PROJECT:	TENAYA MARRIOTT	**PAGE** 1 **OF** 1
LOCATION:	STANDARD GUESTROOMS	5/30/89 S7-DA/S7-D
		DATE **ITEM#**

ITEM: Bedspread, King Special

QUANTITY: 72

SUPPLIER: To Be Determined

MODEL: Throw Style, Round Corners

FINISH: 8 oz. poly fill, cotton back, 4" channel quilt

SIZE: To Fit Bed 72 x 80, 20-21" Drop and 20" Pillow Tuck

SUPPLIER: Schumacher

PATTERN: Spanish Colonial Tapestry

COLOR: Plum

CONTENT: 58% Linen/42% Cotton*

WIDTH: 54"

REPEAT: 25 1/4" Vertical

UNIT YARDAGE: 11 1/2 Approximate

TOTAL YARDAGE: 828 Yards

See S7-D and S7-Da for fabrication specifications.

* Linen-Look/cotton fabric will be considered.

10

RESTAURANT AND HOTEL INTERIORS
710 TERMINAL TOWER, CLEVELAND, OHIO 44113 (216)241-8450

Bedspreads

1. All bedspreads and coverlets are to be machine quilted, style as specified on purchase order.

2. All bedspreads and coverlets are to be pattern matched. All spreads will have a full width panel of fabric centered on the top of the bed. Overall fabric width required to make a one piece cover is as follows:

	Fabric Width	Yards Required
Double	107"	7 3/4 Yards
King Special	127"	11 1/2 Yards

3. All fill will be bonded polyester and weight 8.8 ounces per running yard of 54" goods: equals 8 ounces per running yard of 48" material.

4. Backing material to be approximately 50/50 cotton and polyester blend bleached white.

5. Mattress sizes, side drops, pillow tucks and finished sizes are as follows:

	Width		Length		Drop	Pillow Tuck	Finished Size
Double	54"	x	80"	x	20"	20"	94" x 120"
King Special	72"	x	80"	x	20"	20"	112" x 120"

6. Both corners at tops of bedspreads and coverlets will have the corners mitered on an overlock machine prior to hemming.

7. All bedspreads and coverlets will have a three-quarter inch (3/4") flat hem, single needle lockstitched.

8. Top quilting thread will be #23 nylon, bobbin thread will be size 102 multifilament nylon. All quilting will be lockstitched.

9. All seams will be overlocked with a safety stitch using cotton thread.

10. Hems will be sewn using 30/3 cotton needle thread and #7 monofilament bobbin thread. All hems will be lockstitched.

11. All loose end threads will be neatly trimmed.

12. All bedspreads and coverlets will be individually packaged in plastic bags prior to being put into shipping cartons.

13. A mandatory law label annotating the size of the bedspread or coverlet will be sewn into the top hem.

10

Measuring for Window Treatments

How to Measure for Draperies

Diagram A

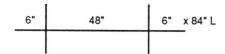

| 6" | 48" | 6" x 84" L |

$$\begin{array}{rl}
\dfrac{12}{60"} = & 6" \text{ on either side of window opening} \\[4pt]
+\ \dfrac{6"}{66"} = & \text{overlap (3" each side)} \\[2pt]
 & \text{Size of Sheer} \\[4pt]
+\ \underline{18"} & 6" \text{ allowance on either side of return and 3" for} \\
 & \text{each side of overlap} \\[4pt]
84" = & \text{Size of Overdrape}
\end{array}$$

When using a valance with a sheer and overdrape, the valance size is the total width of the rod plus 9" return on each side. In the above example, 18" is added to the 60" width to give an overall 78" total width.

Diagram B

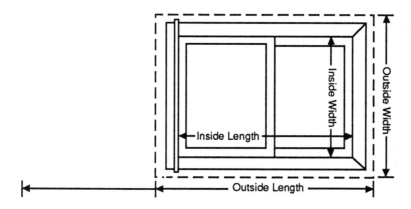

Diagram C

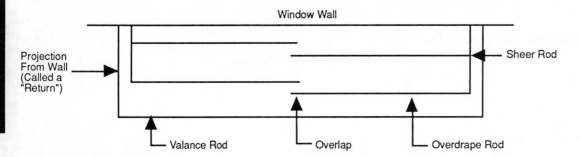

Review Diagram A, B, and C. This is a simple and useful way of measuring for draperies. Wood moulding to wood moulding (OM or outside Mount) is 48". We'd like to extend the draperies 6" further. (Standard is 4" above window frame to hide heading of drape from outside) to 1/2" to 1/4" above carpet nap. The sheer drape is mounted 3" from window, overdrape 6" from window, valance 9" projection from window. There is a 3" overlap (total of 6") on each drape that meets in center.

Diagram D

This diagram shows the three most often used styles for guestroom draperies.

How to Measure Inside Mount or Outside Mount Blinds

Inside Mounting (IM) jamb to jamb for window or door or wall to wall give exact width and mark IM. Measure length in three (3) places, stipulating the shortest length as the required length for your vanes. Do not make allowances. Factory will make all adjustments. In the manufacturing process, we compensate for the length required for the track by cutting 1-1/2" from the length of the vane. Note: You must have a minimum depth of 2-3/4" to accommodate the proper rotation of the vanes.

Outside Mounting (OM) measure exact area to be covered—verticals should overlap window and door frames by at least 3" on each side for a better appearing installation. There should also be 1-1/2" above molding at top of frame for track and brackets. Except for ceiling mounts where 1/2" allowance should be taken from shortest length for clearance. No deductions will be made by factory. Caution: Use a metal or wood ruler when measuring—do not use cloth tape.

Carpet Specifications

Specifications:	Guestroom Carpet
Style:	Custom/Graphic
Color:	Custom
Width:	12 ft.
Weave:	Tufted cut pile
Stitches/inch:	11.0
Gauge:	1/8"
Pile Height:	.310
Yarn	100% Antron Nylon 3
Ply Yarn:	2-ply continuous filament
Dye Technique:	Skein dyed
Total Weight:	77 ounces
Face Weight:	32 ounces
Primary Back:	Polypropylene
Secondary Back:	Jute
Flammability Requirement:	ASTM-E Class B .450

PROJECT: TENAYA MARRIOTT   **PAGE** __1__ **OF** __2__

LOCATION: MAIN DINING—THE SIERRA CLUB   5/1/88   R8/R8 A&C
                                                  DATE   **ITEM#**

ITEM: Arm Dining Chair

QUANTITY: 44

SUPPLIER: Shelby Williams or Equal

MODEL: #G-1755 Transitional
Imperial Timber Arm Chair

FINISH: Weathered Oak

SIZE: 23" W, 38" H, 26" AH

SUPPLIER: Majilite or Equal for seat
and inside back

PATTERN: Baby Ostrich

COLOR: Desert Sand

CONTENT: Nylon Vinyl

WIDTH:
REPEAT:

UNIT YARDAGE: 1-3/4 Yds Total*

TOTAL YARDAGE:

* Advise quantity of each fabric for 44 chairs
Fabric to be flame retardant. Yardage required is based on plain fabric.
Foam to meet California codes.

**G-1755 Transitional Imperial
Timber Arm Chair**
Foam padded spring seat and foam padded
back. Handcarved hardwood frame.

G-1750 Matching Side Chair

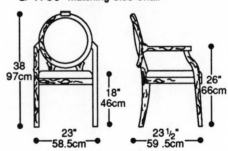

RESTAURANT AND HOTEL INTERIORS
710 TERMINAL TOWER, CLEVELAND, OHIO 44113 (216)241-8450

Case Good Specifications

General Specifications

Wood Species

Exposed solids and veneers shall be scrubbed pine or other approved hardwoods. Unexposed solids shall be sound poplar. All wood solids shall be #1 common grade or better, with no defects affecting strength.

Veneers

Face Veneers—selected good texture, uniform color sliced veneers. Interior Laminating Veneers—selected rotary poplar.

Composition Boards Utilized

Particleboard Specification ANSI A208.1–1979. Hardboard—product standard PS 58–73. Chipcore—50 lbs. density; industrial weight fiberboard. Hardwood Plywood—U.S. Department of Commerce Standard PS-51–71, Type II. All non-solid materials shall be 3 ply construction with a poplar backer.

Moisture Content

All wood is dried to a moisture content of 5–7%. Allows for variation of all climates. Ensures firm bonding joints.

Adhesives

Assembly—all assembly adhesives are specially designed polyvinyl acetates (PVA) for furniture application and will conform to ASTIM D-905 average block shear strength of not less than 2800 lbs. per square inch when tested. Laminating—all laminating adhesives are either urea resins or PVAs.

Finish

Eighteen step finishing material application, plus distressing, incise craving, and 3 step overglazing. Synthetic lacquer shall be applied on all pieces. Wood tops to be finished with alcohol resistant lacquer. Finish sample to be provided for approval. Distressing of wood to be approved by client.

Case Construction

General

Cases are constructed using mortise and tenons, dowelled joints, dust frames, and center guided drawers. Joints are glued and pinned. Cases are reinforced with glue and screwed brace blocks. All case items utilize a moisture resistant barrier composition back panel. Hardboard exposed to the case interior is finished in a manner which compliments the wood finish. Back panel of armoire to be vented for heat release of equipment.

Tops

Matching wood grain high pressure plastic laminate shall be used on desk and nightstand tops. The laminate shall be .050, textured. All cores of tops shall be Novaply or 3 ply particle board, 15/16" thick. Laminate shall be manufactured to match wood finish. Manufacturer:

Drawers

Shall have full dove-tailed construction, French in front, English (conventional) in back. Drawer sides and backs shall be 7/16" laminated oak, sanded smooth and sealed with moisture-resistant drawer coater. Drawer

13

bottoms shall be textured 3-ply 3/16" hardboard, off-white in color, and protected by a clear coat of synthetic lacquer. All case drawers utilize steel, center guided, ball bearing drawer guides with friction stop for positive alignment, stability and smooth operation.

Hardware	To be 2" 0 wrought iron rings and wood pulls (armoire). Samples to be provided for approval.
Glides	All legs shall have 3/4" plastic glides equal to Ronthor-Reiss.
Dust Bottoms	Shall be included at the bottom of all case items.
Headboards	Exposed solids shall be scrubbed pine. Unexposed solids shall be sound poplar. Headboards shall incorporate wall mounting cleats. These shall be designed to wedge headboard tightly against wall by use of mating beveled edges. Headboard cleats shall be wood to measure 48" for 4/6 and 5/0 and 60" for 6/6 headboards.
Armoire	Shall have 270 degree hinged doors. Drawers to have interior center divider panel front to back. Grommeted openings for cord management to be provided along with chimney venting in back panel. Pull out/swivel shelf with 8" extension to be installed for TV. Pull out center shelf to have laminate inset to match wood stain.

Desk Chair Specifications

Materials	Exposed solids shall be scrubbed pine or other approved wood species. Unexposed solids shall be sound poplar or other approved wood species. Seat board shall be three-ply hardwood. Cushion shall be 1–1/4" thick, 4–1/2 pound bonded shredded polyurethane foam.
Seat Construction	Chair cushioning material is polyurethane. It is flame retardant and conforms to any city and state specifications. Chair seat board conforms to fiberboard specifications ANSI A208.3–1980. Slip cushioned seats are removable for easy cleaning and reupholstery. Cushions are attached to the chair frame with non-strippable stove bolts. Wrought iron nail head trim to be applied around seat pad at wood rail.
Frame Construction	Frame shall have four large corner blocks securely glued and screwed. All joints shall be double or triple doweled as size of member permits.
Glides	All four legs shall have 3/4" stainless steel cushion glides.
Finish	As specified for case goods.

13

SPECTRUM SERVICES

| PROJECT: _____ | PAGE_____OF_____ |
| LOCATION: _____ | SPECIFICATIONS |

AREA _____ ROOM TYPE _____ COLOR SCHEME _____

NO. OF ROOMS REQUIRED _____ DESIGNER _____

DATE: _____ REVISION NO. _____ REVISION DATE _____

ITEM NO. AND NAME _____ QTY.: _____

MANUFACTURER _____

SOURCE _____ PAGE NO. _____

MODEL AND SIZE _____

FINISH _____

DRAWING/REFERENCE _____

YARDAGE REQUIRED PER UNIT _____

MANUFACTURER/FABRIC NAME _____

C.O.M. FABRIC NO._____ QTY. _____ REPEAT_____

MANUFACTURER_____ SPECS. _____

P.O. NUMBER: _____
MISC. NOTES:

SAMPLE/COLOR BOARD NO. _____

SHIP TO ADDRESS:

TAG LABEL:

ITEM NO. _____

AREA _____

QUANTITY _____

SAMPLE REQUEST MADE:

RESTAURANT AND HOTEL INTERIORS
710 TERMINAL TOWER, CLEVELAND, OHIO 44113 (216) 241-8450

SPECTRUM
S E R V I C E S

PROJECT: _____   PAGE_____OF_____

LOCATION: _____   SPECIFICATIONS

RESTAURANT AND HOTEL INTERIORS
710 TERMINAL TOWER, CLEVELAND, OHIO 44113 (216) 241-8450

14

SPECTRUM
S E R V I C E S
HOTEL/RESTAURANT DESIGN SPECIALISTS
COMMERCIAL INTERIOR DESIGN

PROJECT

PROJ.#

DATE

REVISION

ITEM#

ITEM

LOCATION: **REF. DRWG.**

ITEM	**MANUFACTURER:**	**QTY.:**
	STYLE:	**SIZE:**
	FINISH:	**MISC.:**
FABRIC	**MANUFACTURER:**	**REPEAT:**
	STYLE:	**WEIGHT:**
	CONTENT:	**YARDAGE EA.:** **TOTAL**

NOTES

14

SAMPLE:

SPECTRUM
S E R V I C E S

SPECIFICATIONS

PROJECT: _____   PAGE _____ OF _____

LOCATION: _____   _____ _____
                                                        DATE   ITEM#

ITEM: SUPPLIER:

QUANTITY: PATTERN:

SUPPLIER: COLOR:

MODEL: CONTENT:

FINISH: WIDTH:

                               REPEAT:

SIZE: UNIT YARDAGE:

                               TOTAL YARDAGE:

RESTAURANT AND HOTEL INTERIORS
710 TERMINAL TOWER, CLEVELAND, OHIO 44113 (216)241-8450

14

SPECTRUM
SERVICES
HOTEL/RESTAURANT DESIGN SPECIALISTS
COMMERCIAL INTERIOR DESIGN

PROJECT	DATE
PROJ. #	REVISION
LOCATION	ITEM #

ITEM	FABRIC COM ☐ MFR. SUPPLIED ☐
QUANTITY	MANUFACTURER
MANUFACTURER	PATTERN #
MODEL #	COLOR
SIZE	CONTENT
FINISH	WIDTH
	REPEAT
	VERT. RPT.
	COST/YD.
	QUANT./PIECE
COST	TOTAL YARDAGE

SAMPLE/SPECIAL INSTRUCTIONS

14

SPECTRUM
S E R V I C E S
HOTEL/RESTAURANT DESIGN SPECIALISTS
COMMERCIAL INTERIOR DESIGN

PROJECT & #	AREA	ITEM	ITEM #

DATE:	REVISION:	DRAWING #:

SPECIFICATION:

BUDGET:	ACTUAL:	QUANTITY:
UNIT COST:	UNIT COST:	SELECTED VENDOR:
		P.O. #:
TOTAL COST:	TOTAL COST:	APPROVAL:
		DESIGNER:
		SAMPLE:

14

ROOM FINISH SCHEDULE

ROOM		FLOOR	BASE					WALLS					CEILING			REMARKS
no.	no.	mat'l	N	E	S	W	note	N	E	S	W	note	ht.	mat'l	note	

ADDENDUM

15

MATERIAL SCHEDULE

	no.	Manufacturer/Type	Specifications	Rep.	Remarks
FLOOR					
BASE					
WALLS					
CLG.					

15

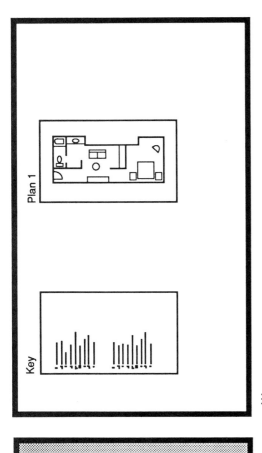

Plan 1

Key

III

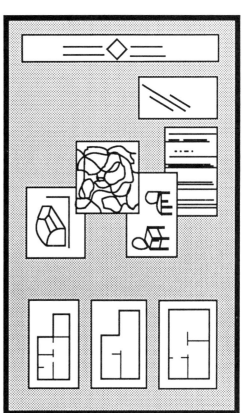

I

II

I. Colorboard framed with double mat.

II. Items on colorboard framed by mat (window pane effect)

III. Typical back side of colorboard with key of items on front of board and plan of the room.

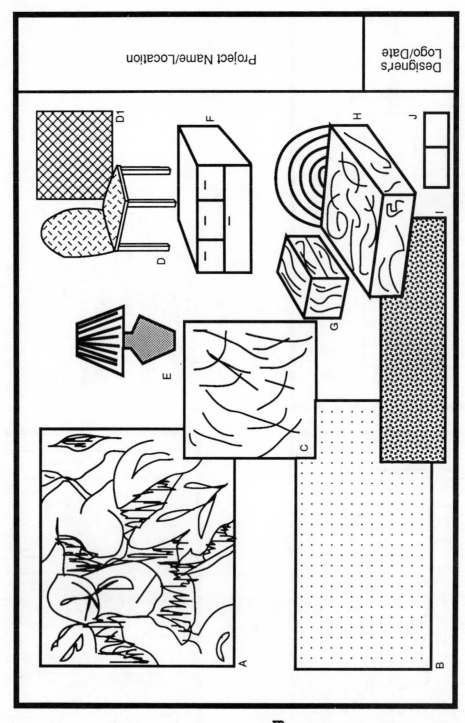

Designer's
Logo/Date

Project Name/Location

A. Bedspread
B. Wallcovering
C. Drapery
D. Chair
D-1. Upholstery
    for chair
E. Lamp
F. Credenza
G. Nightstand
H. Headboard
I. Carpet
J. Paint trim
    selection

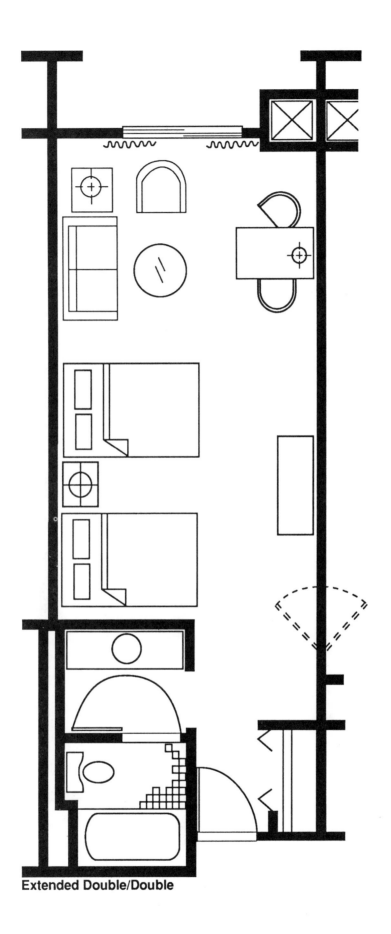

Extended Double/Double

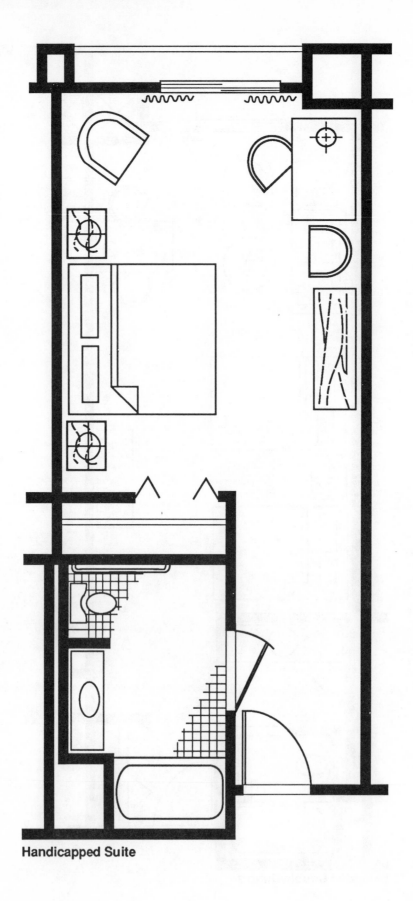

Handicapped Suite

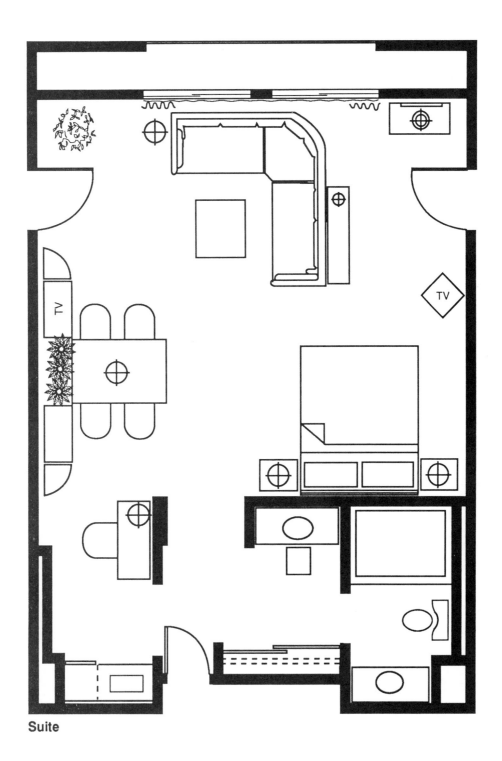

Suite

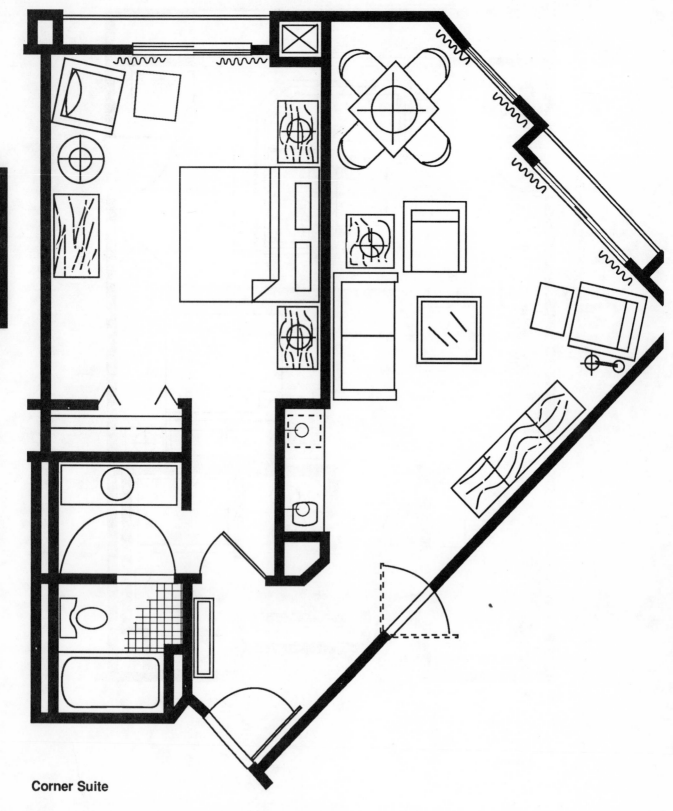

Corner Suite

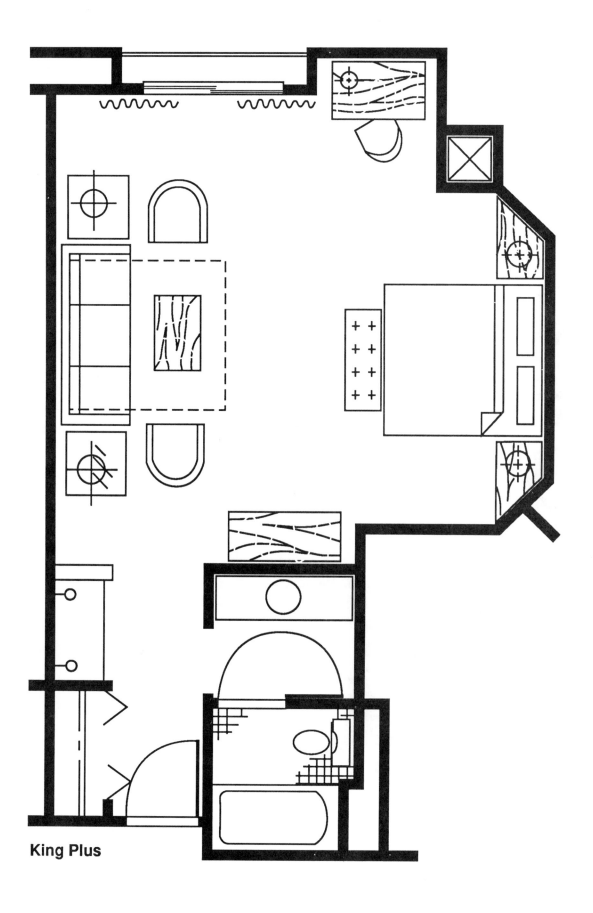

King Plus

17

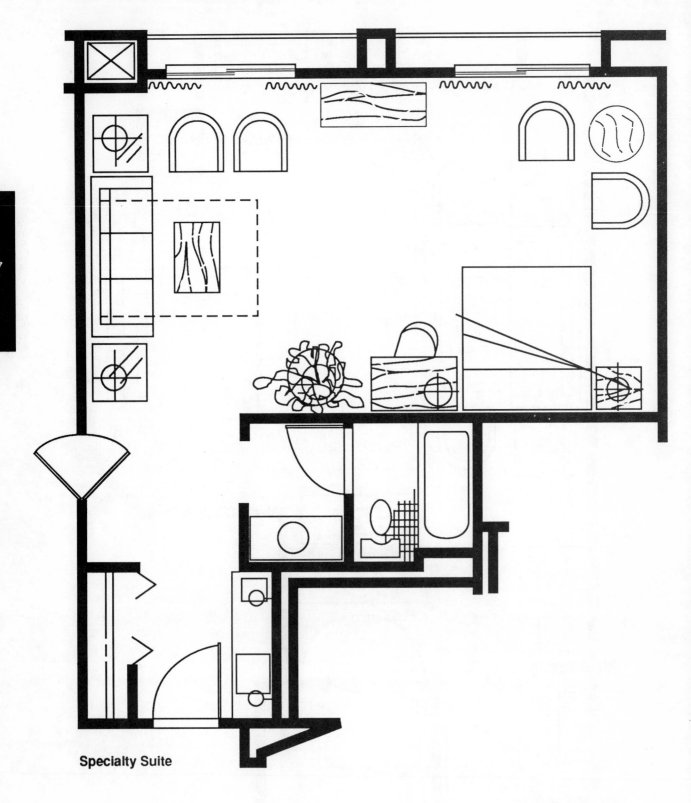

Specialty Suite

17

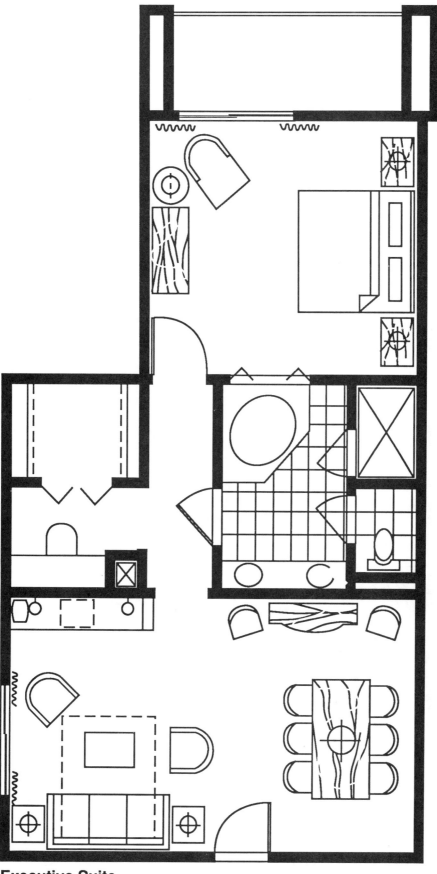

Executive Suite

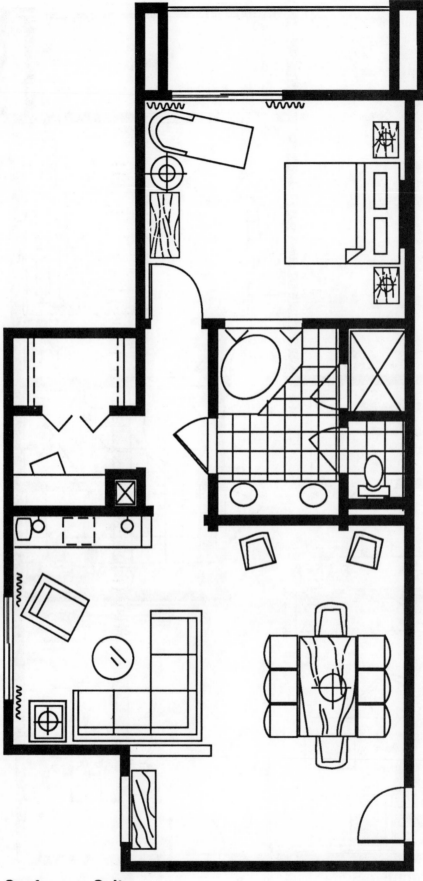

Conference Suite

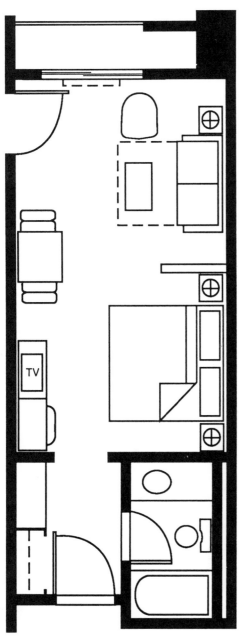

King Suite

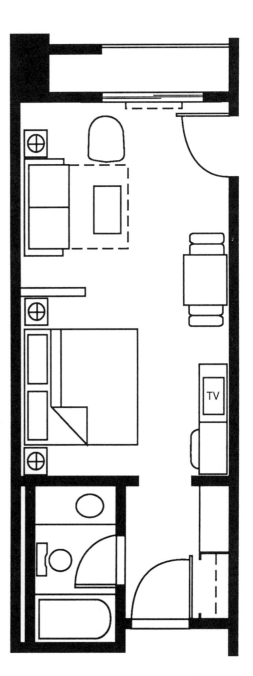

17

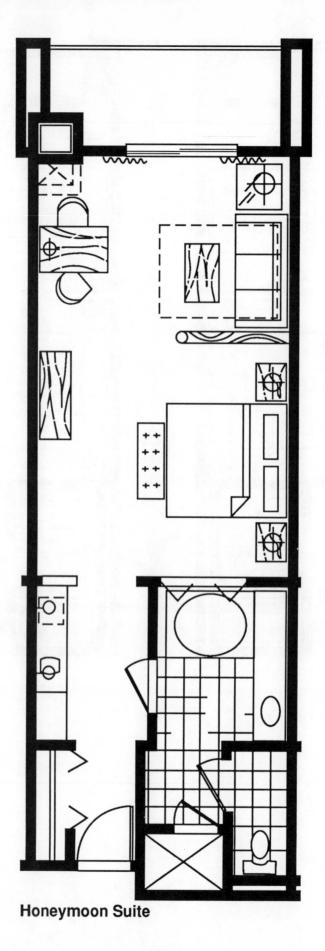

Honeymoon Suite

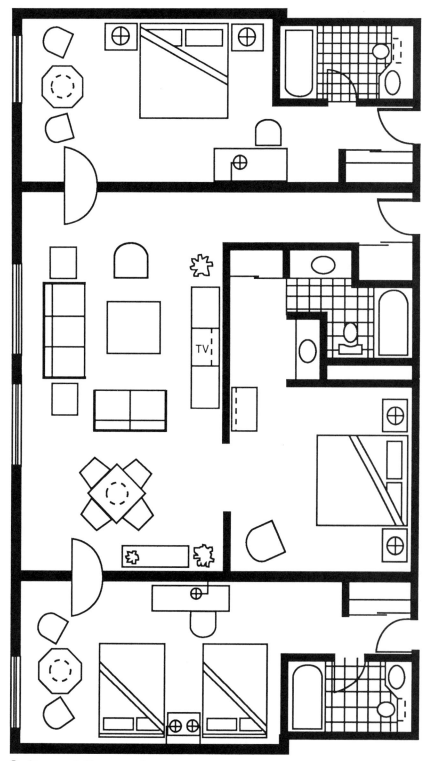

Suite and Connector

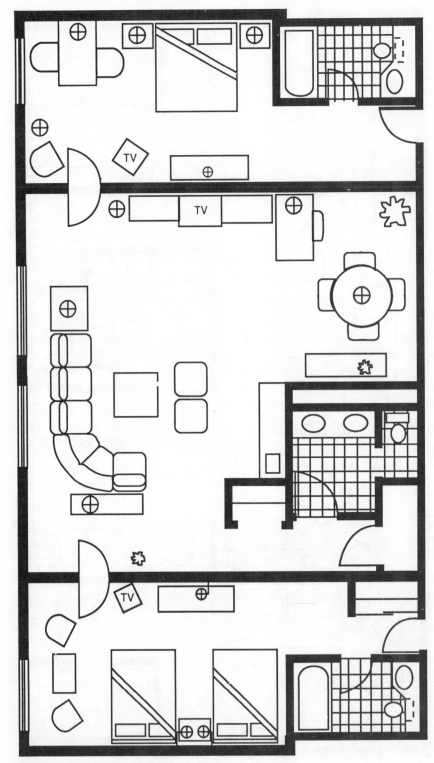

Suite and Connector

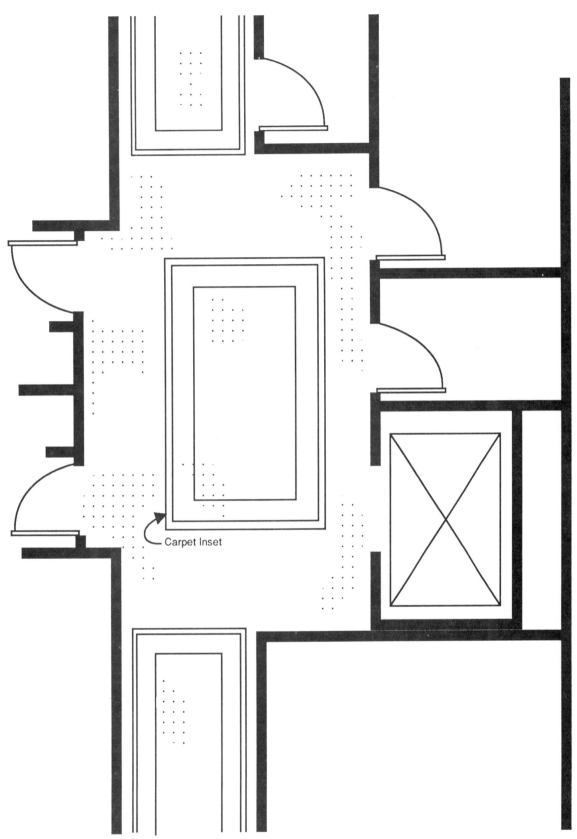

Corridor Carpet Layout

Carpet Inset

Room Number Signage

A. Process Black C
B. 4645 C (Brown)
C. 209 C (Burgandy)
D. 319 C (Blue-green)
E. Yellow C
F. White

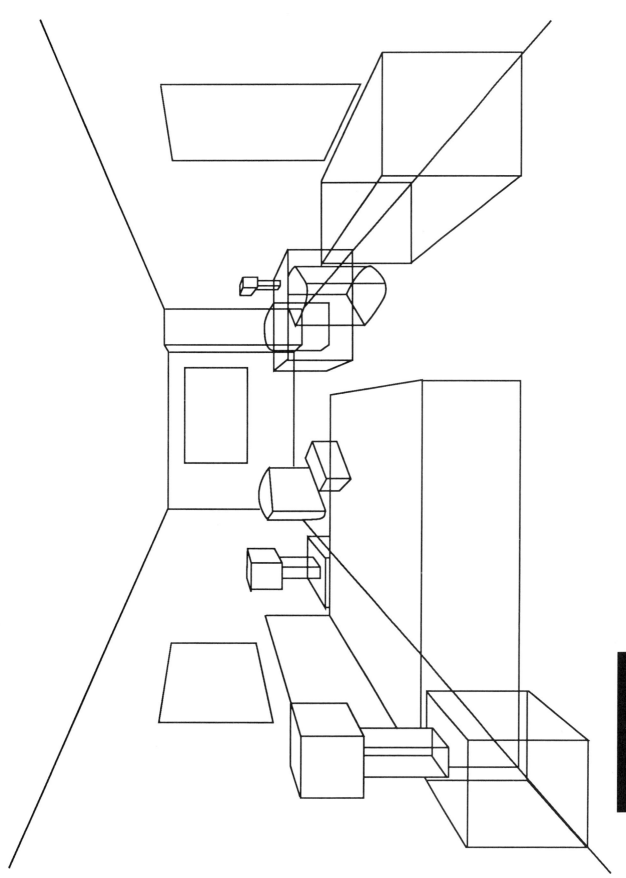

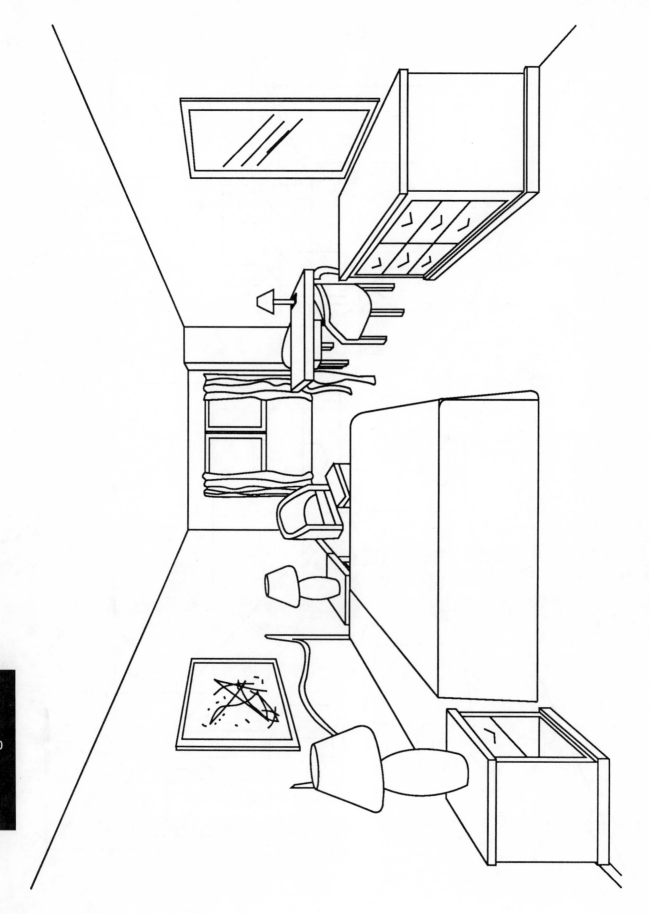

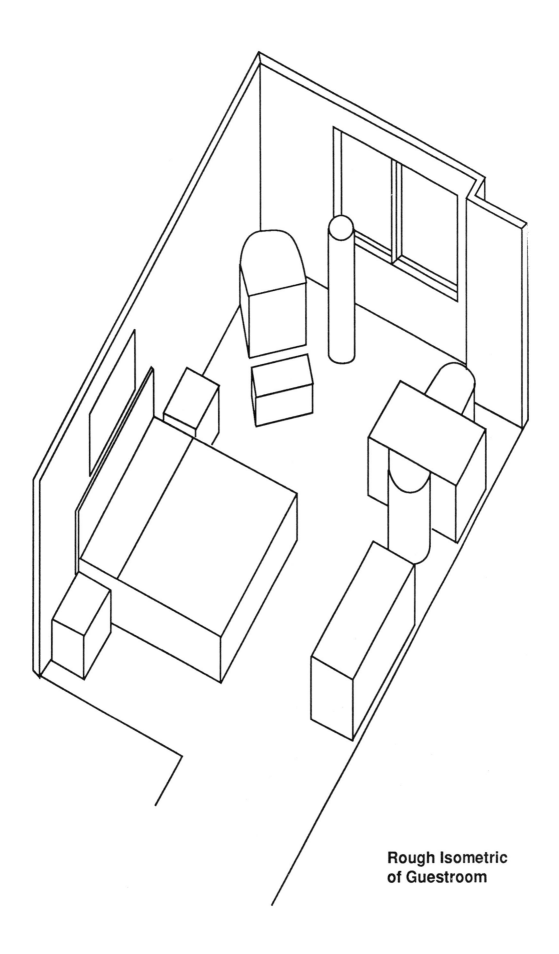

**Rough Isometric
of Guestroom**

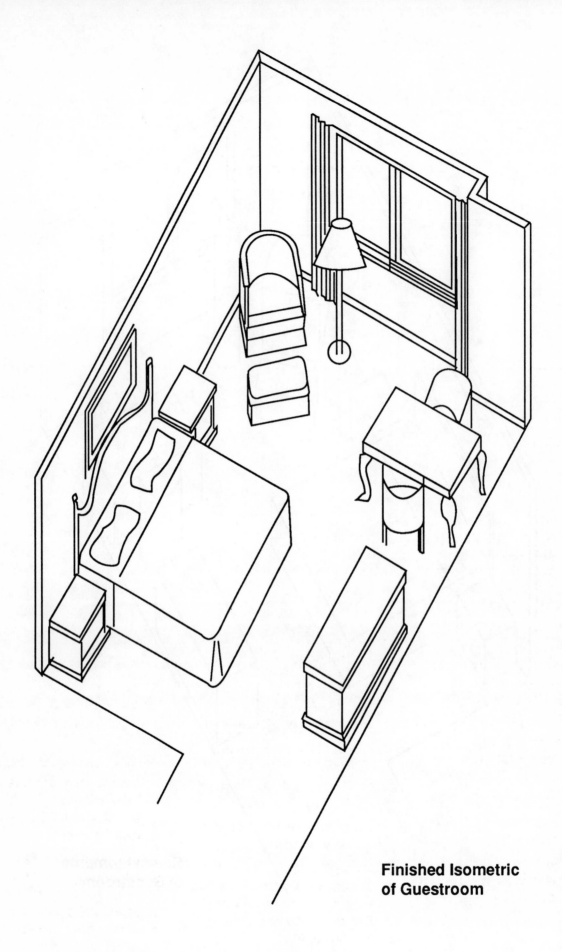

**Finished Isometric
of Guestroom**

Glossary

A.F.F.
Above finished floor measurement.

Accessories
Additional items used to accent i.e. artwork, plants, etc.

Acrylic
Any group of synthetic fibers derived from a compound of hydrogen cyanide and acetylene, and made into fabrics. Acrylics are known to be stain resistant and very durable.

Agglomerate
To gather into a mass i.e. agglomerate marble is fused pieces of matter to make one piece.

Allowance
Additional yardage requirements

Amenity
Anything that adds to one's comfort; convenience.

(ASID)
American Society of Interior Designers

Ballpark Figure
An approximated dollar amount; cost.

Bearing Wall
Main wall in construction that has electrical, water, support columns, etc. within it's structure.

Bedspread Drop
The distance from the top of the mattress to the floor.

Bellowed
When a drapery folds out to make a tenting effect.

Bifolding
2-panel doors secured together by hinges producing a double fold.

Black-Out Drapes
Drapery lined with material that produces a "blackout" of all natural light into the room.

Border Print
Fabric that has a border print on the salvage line.

Casegoods
Furnishings in guestroom with wood or hard surface frames, i.e. dresser, headboard, etc.

Center-Draw
Draperies that separate in the middle and draw to both sides.

Chain Hotel
More than one hotel using the same name.

Channel Quilting
Horizontal or vertical line stitching in continuous lines with a space in between.

Circuit Breaker
A device that automatically interrupts the flow of an electric current, when the current becomes excessive.

Coefficient
Codes determining the amount of slip guard on a tile surface.

Color Board
A presentation piece that includes samples of FF&E; used to describe the style or theme of a project.

Concierge Guestroom
Guestrooms located on a separate floor; known to be upgraded and provide special amenities to the guests. The

room night charge is normally greater than that of a standard guestroom.

Connecting Door
A door located on the interior of a guestroom that adjoins two rooms together.

Convenience Outlet
Electrical outlet located in an accessible area.

Corian
A non-porous solid surface material use in a wide variety of interior application such as countertops, sinks, work surfaces, etc.

Cornice
A type of drapery treatment, usually made of wood, that is mounted at the top of draperies, of which fabric is stretched on to.

Corridor
A long hall or passageway onto which several rooms open or connect to.

Credenza
A type of sideboard or buffet; can be designed for use as a low dresser unit for storage.

Cut Yardage
Yardage that is being cut from a bolt, when entire bolt is not being used.

Drapery Fullness
Amount of fabric used to determine depth and density of pleats in drapes.

Dyelot
Variation in intensity of color from one batch of fabric to the next, can even appear to be a different color.

Efficiency
A guestroom with limited space and limited amenities.

Elevation
A flat scale drawing of the rear, side or front of a building, interior, etc.

End Panel
A stationary piece of finished drapery fabric used at the end of a window.

Executive Committee
The team of individuals who work directly with the hotel General Manager in operating the hotel.

Executive Suite
An upscale guestroom, many times featuring separate sleeping, living and dining quarters.

Feasibility Study
A report completed by professionals who determine the practicality and suitability of a hotel site.

Field Measured
Area or space measured in the field by knowledgeable individual such as a carpet layer measures for carpet.

Finish Schedule
Schedule outlining finishes on all areas of the interior space, including north, east, south and west walls, floor and ceiling.

Flame Resistant
Application of chemicals applied to a material to reduce flammability.

Fluorescent
A glass tube that is coated on the inside with a fluorescent substance that gives off light when mercury vapors in the tube are acted upon by electrons from the cathode.

Franchise
The right to market a product or provide a source, often exclusive for a specific area, as granted by a manufacturer or company.

Full Service Hotel
A hotel offering complete food and beverage facilities, meeting areas, ballroom space, pool and other amenities.

Furniture, Fixtures & Equipment (FF&E)
Items that Interior Designers use to make up specifications.

General Manager
Individual in charge of all hotel operations.

Generic
That is not a trademark (general)

Gray Goods
Standard cloth that is used to print on. Available in different weights, warps and qualities.

Guestroom Wings
Section of hotel occupied by guestrooms.

Hardgoods
Same as casegoods, but also includes wood framed items like seating, i.e. chairs, sofas, etc.

Hardwire
Direct electrical wiring into wall, ceiling or floor.

Incandescent
The light that is produced by a filament of conducting material contained in a vacuum and heated by an electrical current.

Independent Hotel
Hotel that is without a franchise or chain affiliation.

J-Box
Direct electrical connection into wall, floor, etc.

Jacks
A plug-in receptacle used to make electric contact, i.e. phone.

Layout
Diagram of facility that includes furnishings.

Limited Service Hotel
Hotel that has minimal or no food and beverage or meeting room facilities.

Objectives
Pertaining to a project; necessary criteria to produce a need.

One-Way-Draw Draperies
Draperies made as panels that move only in one direction to stack in specified areas, such as the stationary side of a sliding glass door.

Outline Quilting
Stitching around a pattern.

Over-Draperies
Heavier drapery, closer to the room, over another drapery (usually a sheer). Must be traverse, side panel, or tie back.

Parabolic Lens
A lens or shield with perforations that fit into a grid usually above fluorescent lighting so the light can shine through the perforations.

Presentation Board
A model of sorts that displays or visually communicates FF&E items of a design.

Reflective Ceiling
This plan designates ceiling location for light fixtures, wallcovering, paint or any additional surface mounted items.

Refurbish
To re-specify and install new FF&E in a facility.

Rendering
A perspective drawing depicting a designer or architect's conception of a finished building or interior.

Return
The portion of drapery on a 90 degree angle that meets the wall and closes out light. Returns are 3", 6" or 9" depending on what treatment is used.

Revision
To change or update, correct, improve, or amend where necessary.

Renovation
To make fresh or almost new again; clean up, replace worn and broken parts; repair to revive or refresh.

Resort
A hotel primarily used for recreation, as on vacation. A resort facility often has additional amenities you might not find in a standard hotel.

Room Mix
Quantities of each style of guestroom.

Scale
The proportion that a model, map etc. bears to the thing that it represents, the ratio between the dimensions of a representation and those of an object.

Signage
An emblem of sorts that includes letters, symbols, or characters to produce verbage.

Soft Good
Fabric or textile items, i.e. bedspread, carpet, drapes, etc.

Specification
The act of specifying as to actual product, regarding quality, size, performance, terms, finish, etc.

Specification Book
Complete package that includes specification sheets for every area or project.

Stack
The section of a drapery that folds back after the drapery has been traversed open.

Stack Back
Area covered by drapery when drapery is fully opened.

Stack Pleat
Drapery pleats that stack against wall or other surface.

Suite Concept
Alternate guestroom layout, often featuring separate living, dining and sleeping areas.

Template
Tool for drafting/drawing objects.

Tight Seat Back
Upholstered back of chair is secured and permanently mounted.

Tone-on-Tone
A pattern within a fabric of the same color as the background of the fabric.

Tub Enclosure
One piece molded unit that includes three walls and the tub.

Valance
Horizontal top treatment to conceal rod and give a finished appearance to window.

Wall Sconce
Wall mounted light fixture.

Wallmount Lamp
Lamp that is permanently secured to a wall for usage.

Warped
The yarn that runs vertically or lengthwise in woven goods.

Wool
Very absorbent yarn spun from the fibers of the fleece of sheep.